The Story of
GRAND CANYON RAILWAY
Cowboys, Miners, Presidents, and Kings

AL RICHMOND

Grand
Canyon
Association

I could not have written this history
without the help and support of many people.
I dedicate this book to those who willingly gave of
their time and knowledge, and especially to those who
lived this history and are no longer with us.

GRAND CANYON ASSOCIATION

Founded in 1932, Grand Canyon Association is the
National Park Service's official nonprofit partner,
providing private funding to enable Grand Canyon
National Park to raise the margin of excellence
for educational programs and preservation, build
innovation in park services, and support the
necessities not currently funded by federal dollars.
Grand Canyon Association works to inspire people to
protect and enhance Grand Canyon National Park for
present and future generations. Proceeds from the sale
of this book directly support the mission of
Grand Canyon National Park.

Grand Canyon Association
P.O. Box 399, Grand Canyon, AZ 86023
(800) 858-2808
www.grandcanyon.org

© 2017 Grand Canyon Association
Text © 2017 Al Richmond

Composed and printed in the United States of America

New Edition
21 20 19 18 17   1 2 3 4 5

Edited by Faith Marcovecchio
Designed by David Jenney Design

ISBN 978-1-934656-91-4

Library of Congress Cataloging-in-Publication Data pending

COVER PHOTOGRAPH: WILLIAM DIEHL © 2017
BACK COVER PHOTOGRAPHS: COURTESY OF GRAND CANYON
NATIONAL PARK MUSEUM COLLECTION

CONTENTS

This Santa Fe advertisement appeared in *Harper's Weekly* in February 1908, during the first decade of passenger service to the Grand Canyon.

Train crews like this one brought dignitaries and tourists to
Grand Canyon in the 1910s and 1920s.

PREFACE

THIS IS NOT AN INVENTORY OF SIXTY-FOUR MILES OF track, ties, and spikes. It's a recognition of the people, events, circumstances, culture, and equipment that made up, and continue to make up, the daily operation of the Grand Canyon Railway. The line became a part of a larger railroad, and instead of being swallowed by the system, supported it thanks to the notoriety of its destination.

Cowboys, miners, presidents, and kings all played a part in the making of this railroad. Yet these are only a few of the many people from vastly different backgrounds who built, worked for, worked around, worked with, depended on, or rode this line. The Grand Canyon Railway, which transported people and goods from Williams to the Grand Canyon, had a life of its own from the start. It lived in the hearts of the people around it. When it shut down in 1968 because of dwindling revenues, it never really died, for the railroad continued to live in the memories of those who had been close to it.

In 1989, the Grand Canyon Railway was reborn, and today it's writing new history. New friends and memories are being made as the railway rides the rails into its second 100 years.

This early train ticket, dated October 27, 1900, was issued just months after the Santa Fe and Grand Canyon Railroad began operation. The train took passengers as far as Anita Junction, where they boarded a stage-coach for the remainder of the trip.

City of Williams about 1900 with Santa Fe Pacific yards in the foreground.

GETTING UP STEAM

MILLIONS OF YEARS BEFORE humans walked the earth, geologic and climatic forces combined to shape one of the Seven Natural Wonders of the World, the Grand Canyon. A major upheaval produced by tectonic forces, rapid downcutting by an ancient river system, volcanic episodes, and generations of biological changes to flora and fauna became a part of the attraction that draws millions of people to its rim every year.

Because of its immensity and precipitous flanks, the canyon became either a home or a barrier to its first human inhabitants. Spanish conquistadors "discovered" it in the sixteenth century and recorded for posterity its location and their feelings of awe. From that time until the late 1800s, the Grand Canyon remained unexplored, a blank spot on maps of North America. It lay far removed from population centers and major routes of travel. Major John Wesley Powell's two voyages of exploration on the Colorado River through the Grand Canyon, in 1869 and 1871–72, changed all of that. His reports and newspaper articles describing his travels brought attention to the Colorado Plateau and the Grand Canyon. In effect, Powell's expeditions opened the region to further exploration and settlement.

During the sequences of deposition and erosion that formed the canyon, vast stores of mineral wealth were incorporated into this most marvelous of landscapes. In turn, climate exposed them. Sequences of freezing, thawing, and erosion by wind and water gave early prospectors a brief glimpse into the riches awaiting those smart and strong enough to get at them. The canyon and the region to its south held rewards for the industrious and tricks for the unwary.

By the 1880s, people began to realize the potential of this diverse landscape and tap its resources. Ranchers and prospectors moved into the region. Cattle and sheep thrived on its grasses. The Francis Mining District, established fifteen miles south of Grand Canyon, became a classic scene of newcomers searching for instant riches. Hardworking men knew fortunes existed in (and on) the earth, and many did their best to retrieve them. In later years, others would mine the pockets of tourists who flocked to the rim in greater numbers with each passing year.

In the late 1800s, many questions plagued prospectors, ranchers, legislators, and others seeking their fortunes. How could they unlock the mineral wealth of the Francis Mining District? How would they get cattle and sheep to market? How might they attract people to the Grand Canyon? Only one solution made any sense: a railroad.

The problem was that in the early 1880s, railroads did not exist in northern Arizona. Until then, travel had been by horse, mule, foot, wagon, or stagecoach. Even camels made their way across the scene in the 1850s, when Lieutenant Edward F. Beale surveyed the area. Travelers to the Grand Canyon in these early years had no fast and easy means of transportation.

Anyone shipping cattle or sheep drove them many miles to railheads, which was none too profitable. A prospector who had found what he believed to be instant wealth soon realized he could not ship his ore except by wagon. No profit there either. Very few tourists traveled to the Grand Canyon in those early days, and those who did found horses and wagons to be the only means available for the several-day round-trip from Flagstaff, Williams, or Ash Fork. These arrangements brought small returns for livery and stage operators and proved to be very tiresome for travelers.

When the Atlantic and Pacific Railroad made its way into the area in the summer of 1882, it represented a great improvement in transportation for the residents

Westbound passenger train pulling into the original Williams Depot and freight house circa 1905. Both structures were moved in 1907 to the south side of the tracks and are currently the Williams Visitor Center.

of the region. However, this east-west enterprise had no intention of going to the Grand Canyon.

Certainly the Atlantic and Pacific made it easier for the ranchers, who now only had to drive their cattle and sheep to the nearest loading point on the main line. Every reduction in distance saved time, money, and helped to ensure the animals arrived at market in better condition. Miners could haul their ore to the main line now too, considerably reducing transportation costs so they finally made a small profit. Tourists remained the only group that didn't benefit.

Everyone sensed there was money to be made at the canyon. Promoters could smell it. They soon put pressure on the governor and the legislature. "The territory of Arizona needs more railroads!" became the cry of the day. "There's money in the ground and the only way to get it out is by railroad!"

Jumping on the bandwagon in 1887 (as if it had any choice in the matter), the 15th Arizona Territorial Legislature exempted any company building a railroad in Arizona from paying property taxes for six years. The lawmakers even specifically mentioned a railroad from the Atlantic and Pacific line to the Grand Canyon. This incentive interested a few people and railroads were built, but not in northern Arizona. Tourism to the Grand Canyon did not seem like something profitable and besides, plenty of other mines operated in central and southern Arizona. The livery, stage, and freight companies could handle the existing traffic. Why bother to spend

William Owen "Buckey" O'Neill, captain in the Rough Riders. This photo was taken in New York, just prior to O'Neill's departure for Cuba.

the money?

But when prospectors from the Francis Mining District started showing up at assay offices with copper ore richer than any ever seen in Arizona, people began to change their minds. U.S. Senator William Andrew Clark of the United Verde Copper Company, which had vastly rich holdings in Jerome, became a proponent of a railway, and soon his engineers began to stake claims in the Francis District.

For in the early 1890s, copper was king in Arizona. Enthusiastic stories of gold and silver mines also appeared in the press, but copper remained the big money maker because copper ore is far more abundant and easier and less expensive to mine than gold or silver. Still, no one jumped at the chance to build a railroad to the canyon. Even with someone like Senator Clark expressing interest, there was a general reluctance to part with investment capital for the railroad.

About 1893, William O. "Buckey" O'Neill, son of Ireland, mayor of Prescott, legendary sheriff of Yavapai County, prospector, promoter, and later one of Teddy Roosevelt's Rough Riders, realized money could be made in the mining and railroad business between Williams and the Grand Canyon. He had a number of good claims and backed some others in what would become the Anita area. Several were in the Grand Canyon proper, and O'Neill built a substantial cabin on the South Rim that still stands today. But to get at this wealth, he needed money for development, and there wasn't enough financial backing in the vicinity to buy a good bottle of whiskey. Or so it seemed.

O'Neill began to check around. Virtually all of the big available money was back east. That being the case, he packed up his ore samples and headed for the eastern financial districts. He knocked on a lot of doors with little or no success until he came across the investment firm of Lombard, Goode and Company in New York. This relatively small investment firm did enough business to have offices in Chicago and London too. O'Neill found them to be receptive but not overly enthusiastic.

Thomas Lombard, who had not been any farther west than Chicago, was taken by O'Neill's open manner, his stories of the Wild West, and his descriptions of the beauty and riches of Grand Canyon. O'Neill made several trips to New York and Chicago in the next several years to try to consolidate a deal with the company, but most of his progress was limited to becoming a family friend of the Lombards.

Despite initial setbacks in New York, somehow O'Neill convinced enough small investors in the Williams area to come up with $1,000 to pay for a preliminary survey of the railroad. Crews completed the survey in 1894, and O'Neill again went to see Thomas Lombard. This time, he convinced Lombard of the need for a personal inspection. The eastern businessman made his first trip to the area in 1895, and O'Neill gave him and his party a royal tour of the region. Lombard was not in the physical condition required of such an arduous trip and tired easily. But he came away thoroughly impressed. Now he had to convince the conservative men at his company to get involved, and they were not very willing to risk a buck.

J. DuPratt White (left) and Buckey O'Neill (right), watch Thomas Lombard cook dinner in a silver chafing dish at the Grand Canyon during their 1895 visit.

Thanks to O'Neill's enthusiasm, Lombard had become convinced of the venture's sound potential, and the scenic beauty of the Grand Canyon captivated him. Still, his measured enthusiasm didn't raise any capital for the project. In his plodding way, Lombard spent several years trying to secure enough solid investors to make the railroad go. Eventually, Lombard, Goode and Company formed the Tusayan Development Company to develop their several mining claims, a move that provided an aura of respectability to the venture.

Next, O'Neill and Lombard went to see E. P. Ripley, president of the Atchison, Topeka and Santa Fe Railroad, to try to sell him on the idea. But they could not get him to invest the Santa Fe's money in their proposal. Ripley considered Lombard, Goode and Company to be a fly-by-night organization and their project a bluff. For years, he reiterated these sentiments in his correspondence with subordinates. His opinion probably led to the demise of the original railroad project more than any other factor.

Oddly enough, in spite of Ripley's opinion of the investment firm, Thomas Lombard's partner, Lowry Goode, kept up a good rapport with the chairmen of the boards of the Atchison, Topeka and Santa Fe Railroad and the Santa Fe Pacific Railroad. Cordial letters between Goode and Aldace F. Walker expressed positive sentiments about completion of the line. Their relationship helped to keep the project moving forward.

Correspondence from O'Neill—and rich ore samples he sent Walker and Ripley in 1897—finally proved persuasive. In a letter written September 10, 1897, on stationery from the Office of the Mayor of Prescott, O'Neill listed the samples sent by express that day:

Two samples of asbestos
Sample of red ochre mineral paint
Sample of yellow ochre mineral paint
Sample of mica
Samples of lead and silver ore
Samples of gold bearing rock—sulphurets
Sample of copper ore

He described the contents as follows:

All…are from the Grand Canyon of the Colorado, and all…are found in large quantities. The copper ore I limited to one specimen as I understood from you in Flagstaff that you already had specimens of this rock. As this is a particularly fine sample though I thought it might interest you.

When considering the benefits and potential of his railroad, however, O'Neill envisioned far more than mining; he also foresaw the possibilities of tourist travel to the South Rim. To this end, he wrote:

I also send you a small map showing points in the Canyon which have heretofore received little attention, notably the very magnificent waterfalls, among them Rainbow falls 1600 feet high, Mooney's Falls 265 feet and others. It also shows points of interest such as the Cathedral Cave 3200 feet deep, Echo Cliffs, the various named peaks of greatest prominence, etc., my idea being that if incorporated in the folders of the Santa Fe it would give the Canyon… individuality and attractiveness that it does not now possess for the ordinary traveller who regards it when looking at the map as merely a barren waste. As the Santa Fe has a kind of proprietary interest in the Canyon greater than anyone else, I think it should be willing of accepting the responsibility of sta[ge]ing for it. Really though the Canyon is a gold mine in the way of money-making for the Sa[n]ta Fe, and why it has never been recognized and worked as such I am at a loss to conceive.

Although O'Neill had an apparent need for either a new typewriter or a secretary, his letter clearly showed that his thoughts for the railroad extended beyond mining interests.

In 1897, Lombard and Goode made a survey of the proposed line. At that time, they estimated a cost of $10,000 per mile for construction. This figure, O'Neill said to Walker, "is far in excess of what I had figured on."

Lombard and O'Neill kept plugging away. By 1897, they had continued to secure enough investors, many of them small businessmen from Williams and vicinity, to get things started. These included R. R. Coleman, Frank and August Polson, Max Salzman, George U. Young, James Walsh, the J. M. Dennis Lumber Company, the Arizona Central Bank, and later the Saginaw and Manistee Lumber Company. The major hurdles for the Santa Fe and Grand Canyon Railroad were its methods of financing and the issuance of bonds. These remained to be haggled over until 1898.

Reports from a variety of sources indicate that the investors from Williams put about $200,000 toward the project. For the businessmen of this small community to make such a large financial commitment to the railroad speaks volumes about its need and potential.

Polson family in Sweden with August (TOP LEFT) and Frank (THIRD FROM TOP LEFT), taken in 1883.

A big boost came when the 19th Arizona Territorial Legislature reestablished the then-expired property tax incentives for building railroads initially passed in 1887. Finally convinced that enough investment money existed, Lombard, Goode and Company incorporated the Santa Fe and Grand Canyon Railroad Company on July 31, 1897, with Lowry W. Goode as president.

In O'Neill's hometown

George U. Young, publisher and editor of the *Williams News*. He recovered only $500 of his large investment in the Santa Fe and Grand Canyon Railroad.

of Prescott, the progress was duly reported in the August 11 issue of the *Arizona Weekly Journal-Miner*:

Plans have been perfected for a railroad to the Grand Canyon of the Colorado, and construction is to begin from a point on the Santa Fe Pacific at Flagstaff or Williams. A tenth of the million dollar capital stock is already on hand, and the bonds of the line are being placed in the east. The enterprise is backed by Lombard, Goode & Co., of Chicago, and is under the management of Mayor O'Neill, of Prescott. The new line will be known as the Santa Fe and Grand Canyon Railroad and will be 72 miles in length, and will tap the canyon at the head of the Bright Angel trail. At that point is proposed the erection of a large hotel. Mr. O'Neill is now in the east in the interest of his railroad scheme.

Elmer Duffield (seated), an early Santa Fe trainmaster, and family.
RIGHT: Frank and Florida Polson on their wedding day, 1891.

Mayor O'Neill has gone up to Williams and other points on the Santa Fe Pacific, to meet a party of eastern capitalists whome [*sic*] he has interested in the building of the new railroad to the Grand Canyon. The building of the road has been definitely settled, and the route is to be decided on. Williams and Flagstaff are lively competitors for it, but the former is said to have the preference, being more direct, and having in addition an easier grade and being less in distance. A force of men will be put to work inside of a week surveying and grading.

The company also applied for and received a right-of-way across the Coconino National Forest Reserve. As recorded with the Coconino County Recorder, the right-of-way would run "north to Lombard on the rim of the Grand Canyon of the Colorado River, a distance of 65 miles from Williams at the Santa Fe Pacific Railroad." Note the reference to "Lombard." Had Lombard's company completed the road to the canyon, what is known as Grand Canyon Village today would have been known as Lombard, Arizona.

Incorporated and with sufficient funds to begin the project, the Santa Fe and Grand Canyon Railroad became a force to be reckoned with. Newspapers of the region carried stories of its progress and documented the competition between the various factions. The *Journal-Miner* reported the progress in its October 13, 1897, issue:

It took another several months, but during November and December 1897 and January 1898, the survey, under the skilled hands of surveyor William Lockridge, was completed. Recorded in Coconino County is an affidavit of commencement of actual construction, a legal document necessary to comply with the requirements of the territorial legislature's tax exemptions. It states in part, "between 24th day of February and 3rd day of March 1898 completed grading on

Surveyor W. H. Lockridge, (**CENTER**) with his chainmen J. Durane (**RIGHT**) and J. Randall (**LEFT**) in 1900 with the tools of their trade.

1650 feet of railroad from the Williams station east and northerly...moving 1050 6/10 cubic yards in earth excavation, earth embankment and loose rock." To any interested parties, these recorded milestones were assurances of the railroad's reality. However, the signing of far more important documents occurred in New York on December 16, 1897.

A joint use agreement between the Santa Fe Pacific Railroad and the Santa Fe and Grand Canyon Railroad for the station grounds in Williams was signed and became effective that day. It gave the line needed access from the main line to the northbound track. Probably the most important conditions of the agreement, however, were the water delivery provisions. The cost specified was $1 for every engine tank of 3,500 gallons or less, with water for "other than engine purposes" to be charged at the rate of 30¢ per 100 gallons (later amended to 1,000 gallons). If water became unavailable in Williams, the Santa Fe Pacific agreed to haul water from its wells at Bellemont or Ash Fork at the rate of $15 per 5,000 gallons. E. P. Ripley signed for the Santa Fe Pacific and William O. O'Neill signed as the vice president for the Santa Fe and Grand Canyon Railroad.

A joint tariff agreement effective December 31, 1897, brought legitimate business recognition from the rest of the railroad world. Upon completion of the line, it said,

Freight and passengers shall be routed upon through joint tariff rates from all points upon any railroad owned or leased and operated by either of the Santa Fe Companies, to all points on the line of the Grand Canyon Company; and in a like manner all freight and passengers shall be routed upon through joint

The Santa Fe masonry dam south of Williams. It served as the primary source of water for the railroad and town, and continues to serve the City of Williams.

tariff rates from points on the Grand Canyon Railroad to all points on the aforesaid lines of the Santa Fe Companies.

Ripley signed as president for the Santa Fe Pacific Railroad, the Atchison, Topeka and Santa Fe Railway, and Southern California Railway Companies, with O'Neill signing for the Santa Fe and Grand Canyon Railroad.

Certainly there would have been an article in the *Williams News* about the agreements, but no copies survive. However, an article dated December 24, 1897, in an unidentified northern Arizona newspaper stated,

Word is received from Prescott that Bucky [*sic*]

O'Neill has returned from New York, where he had been in the interest of his copper mines and smelter. Bucky says that both the smelter and Grand Canyon railroad are absolutely assured facts, as Lombard, Goode & Company are backing the ventures.

But additional financial arrangements led to delays, and soon O'Neill's project began, once again, to stall. The investors were unsettled when no interest was paid on their money. They knew from previous reports that they were not the only ones interested in putting this railroad through.

As early as 1892, *The Daily Star* of Tucson printed a story of "a force of thirteen teams" beginning work on the Flagstaff and Black Canyon Railroad to proceed from "Cliff Spur, fourteen miles northeast of Flagstaff." It further stated, "The tourist and scientist will no longer be deterred from visiting the wonder of wonders on account of the inconvenience of stage or hack travel, but can ride in a palace car to [the] brink of the grand canyon of the Colorado."

Four years later, on March 10, 1896, articles of incorporation in the territory of Arizona recorded the Globe, Flagstaff and Canyon Railroad "to Cameron Point on the Grand Canyon." This company had been previously incorporated as the Flagstaff and Canyon Railroad Company on June 22, 1895. Eight years before that, on June 16, 1887, the Grand Canyon Railroad Company had been incorporated in Prescott with the intention of building a railroad from Seligman to the canyon. And another company had secured from the 54th Congress a right-of-way from Flagstaff to the Grand Canyon on June 8, 1886.

Articles in the *Flagstaff Sun-Democrat* carried stories of the widespread competition. The editor, in the September 23, 1897, issue, went so far as to state, "It is only a question of a few months till a railroad will be built from Flagstaff to the Grand Canyon, and then the Skylight City will have a substantial growth and a rapid increase in wealth and population. A smelter will be located here."

Naturally the people of Flagstaff could see the benefits of having the railroad run from their city to the South Rim, and the competition must have been intense. To this end, the newspaper articles continued. The October 28 issue carried two lines, "When the Grand Canyon railroad is built, it will be built from Flagstaff," proving that the investors of Williams had direct competition from their neighbors.

Yet even before surveys had been completed, it became obvious the route from Williams presented the best solution. Shorter by at least ten miles, the grade is not as steep as other routes proposed, and Williams had already been designated a division of the main east-west Santa Fe Pacific.

Finally all of the financial components came together to move the Ripley/O'Neill project forward. According to a story in George Young's *Williams News*, roadbed construction commenced on June 1, 1899, with P. F. Randall as chief engineer of construction. For materials, on June 8, L. W. Goode and H. N. Goode incorporated the Canyon Construction Company in the territory of Arizona "to build railroads and all other accessories pertinent to railroads."

This news would have brought joy to the heart of Buckey O'Neill had he known of it, especially after all of the effort, time, and money he had expended. But this was not to be. O'Neill's adventuresome ways had finally caught up with him the previous year.

When Colonel Theodore Roosevelt organized his regiment of Rough Riders at the onset of the Spanish-American War, O'Neill became the first to organize a troop to serve under him. Captain O'Neill assembled a tough group of miners, cowboys, and loggers from the territory of Arizona into Troop A, 1st U.S. Volunteer Cavalry. These men served with great distinction in Cuba and particularly at Kettle Hill (usually reported as San Juan Hill), but not as cavalry. Their horses had been left behind in the United States due to lack of transport. While the men were operating as infantry in preparation for the attack of Kettle Hill, a Spanish sniper took aim at an officer walking up and down in full view, giving encouragement to his men. The marksman adjusted his sights in the half-light of dawn on July 1, 1898, and squeezed his trigger. Buckey O'Neill died doing what he did best—leading men into dangerous places and taking more risks than anyone else. He held the rank of brevet major at the time.

O'Neill had survived many previous encounters with death at the hands of robbers and gunmen. In addition, a raging river had drowned his horse but failed to claim him, and he survived a leap from a moving train to capture an escaped prisoner. His luck ran out in Cuba, however, and even his resourcefulness couldn't overcome this obstacle.

Although O'Neill didn't live to see his efforts on behalf of the railroad come to realization, no one had worked harder to bring a rail line to northern Arizona and the South Rim of the canyon. If any one person is to be thanked or praised for making the Grand Canyon Railway a reality, it is William Owen "Buckey" O'Neill.

By the summer of 1899, another railroad company entered the fray alongside the Santa Fe and Grand Canyon Railroad. This added aggravation came in the form of the Grand Canyon Railway Company of Arizona, which was incorporated on July 8, 1899. The new company planned to build north from Ash Fork, but they ran into even more financing difficulties than Lombard, Goode and Company had.

In addition, E. P. Ripley had decided that the Grand Canyon line would be added to the Santa Fe's roster of companies, and he threw all of the legal roadblocks at his disposal into the path of Lombard, Goode and Company. In no uncertain terms, Ripley stated to W. G. Nevin, his general manager in Los Angeles, that all dealings for rentals and purchases with the Santa Fe and Grand Canyon Railroad would be cash up-front. Chief Engineer Randall had asked for motive power, boarding trains, flatcars, and rails as early as August 15. But they were not immediately forthcoming, and two more months of letters, telegrams, and legal dealings passed back and forth between Williams, Los Angeles, Chicago, and New York before final arrangements for equipment leases and material purchases from the Santa Fe Pacific could be made.

On October 12, 1899, Randall requested from Nevin the following:

Connection at the main line of the SFP with the SF&GC
1 engine, 19 x 26, 10 wheeler
18 boxcars fitted for a boarding train

1 kitchen
1 commissary
6 dining
8 sleepers
1 foreman
1 trainmen [*sic*] and engineers
Coal, water, oil and waste for cars
1 engine additional and 15 flats for running material to the front

Randall figured at that time that his crews had the capability of laying not more than fifty or sixty tons of rail per day, which he asked to be delivered, along with fastenings, at the rate requested on flatcars, if possible. Randall had ordered fifty-six-pound relay rail, but the Santa Fe Pacific shipped both fifty-two and fifty-six pound.

With completion of the financial arrangements and Randall's request approved, Santa Fe Pacific locomotives 49 and 88 moved onto the Grand Canyon line for the first time. Number 49 later became 282, the first regularly scheduled locomotive to the Grand Canyon. In June 1900, Santa Fe Pacific 51 replaced Santa Fe Pacific 88. Both 49 and 51 were of the 4-6-0 configuration, and 88 was a 4-4-0. During the 1900 reorganization of motive power, number 49 was renumbered to 282, 51 became 281, and 88 changed to 125. Locomotives 49/282 and 51/281 had been built by Baldwin, and 88/125 by New York.

Further agreements provided that the Santa Fe Pacific would supply water to the Santa Fe and Grand Canyon Railroad locomotives at 30¢ cents per 1,000 gallons, and that necessary outfit and water cars would be leased

at the rate of $1 per day, as well as one coach at the rate of $2.50 per day and car 204 at $1.50 per day. This last combination car made its initial run on September 17, 1900, with number 282, and it remained in passenger service on the line for many years.

And so the initial business had been completed. The Santa Fe and Grand Canyon Railroad now had its motive power and rolling stock on lease, as well as the materials needed to complete track to the mines and the rim. The contract guaranteed the railroad a price of fifty-six-pound relay rail and fastenings at $25 per ton, plus shipping at 1¢ per ton per mile. But there was a catch: supplies and services had to be paid in Santa Fe and Grand Canyon Railroad gold bonds to Santa Fe at the rate of 60¢ on the dollar. In effect, cost of the rail and fastenings now became $41.26 per ton. As it turned out, with intent by Ripley and foolishness on the part of Lombard and Goode, this literally cut the heart out of the company.

Various supply companies were also paid in bonds. For instance, the company issued forty shares of common stock to purchase three carloads of spikes from the Richmond Standard Steel Spike & Iron Company of Richmond, Virginia. As the bonds became worth less and less, these companies were added to a long list of creditors left holding the bag.

Lombard and Goode never listed these bonds on the stock exchange, and they could only be redeemed with the Santa Fe Pacific. Later on, Ripley cut the value to 40¢, and then to 10¢ on the dollar. At this rate, it did not take too long before the Santa Fe and Grand Canyon Railroad found itself in serious financial condition.

Added to this, lack of water rendered the smelter, run

The Santa Fe railroad yard in 1902 with the station and freight depot up the line and downtown Williams to the left.

by the Anita Consolidated Copper Company, inoperable. Built at the east end of Williams to refine the ore mined at Grand Canyon, the smelter depended on water from the town's Santa Fe Dam, which had been built by the Atchison, Topeka and Santa Fe Railway to supply water to its steam locomotives. Without water, the smelter was useless. Just as Lombard, Goode and Company were expecting to go into operation, they received notification that the Santa Fe Dam had partially washed out and that the remaining water had to go to their own railroad and the town of Williams. The AT&SF would not honor their contract with the Grand Canyon Railway. It seemed most convenient that only enough

water had been lost to "honorably" disallow water use by the smelter, but enough remained for the railway and the town of Williams to operate. Speculation was rife that the railroad company had been involved in the washout.

In spite of these difficulties, railroad construction pushed on to Anita Junction, forty-five miles north of Williams. From here, the 2.87-mile spur to Anita Camp, the mining destination of the railroad, joined the main line. Anita Junction (later Anita), Anita Camp, and the Anita mines all were named after Thomas Lombard's daughter.

On March 15, 1900, the Santa Fe and Grand Canyon Railroad began operation. Copper ore from the mines was carried to Williams via rail for the first time. Passenger service also began. Tourists could now board the train in Williams and travel north to Anita Junction in comfort. At Anita, they would board stagecoaches for the remaining twenty-mile trip to the canyon. The trip had been cut from three days to five and a half hours, as long as the road north from Anita Junction remained in good condition.

A train schedule published in the *Williams News* of June 22, 1901, showed train number 10 leaving Williams for Anita Junction at 12:30 p.m. via Red Lake, Prado, Valle, and Willaha. From there, the stage left at 3:00 p.m., with arrival at the Grand Canyon via Anita and Coconino at 6:00 p.m. The return trip by stage left the Grand Canyon at 1:30 p.m. to meet the train at Anita Junction for a 4:00 p.m. departure to Williams, with

Santa Fe Pacific locomotive No. 49 and combination car No. 204 at Anita Junction in 1900. Note the water tank on the flatcar.

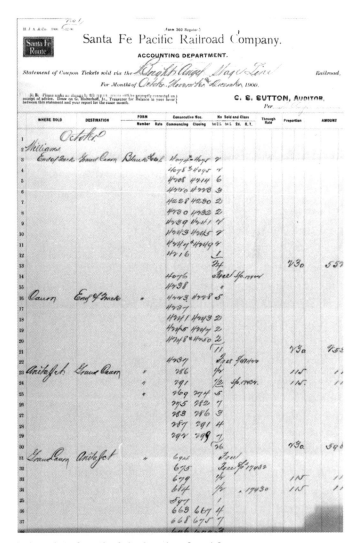

Ledger sheet from the Anita Junction–Grand Canyon stage for October 1900.

scheduled arrival at 6:30 p.m. Most likely, this timetable had been followed from the beginning of service.

What a relief these events must have brought to all parties involved. It doesn't take much imagination to hear the toasts and cheers offered at Anita, Williams, New York, and Chicago. In spite of Ripley's maneuvering, the railroad had succeeded!

With passenger service on the Santa Fe and Grand Canyon Railroad finally a reality, Lombard, Goode and Company turned its energies to the completion of the railroad to the rim. They found success to be a double-edged sword because their remaining capital would only allow them to complete another 8.63 miles.

To add to their woes, the water shortage caused the smelter to remain inoperable, so company officials began to consider alternative facilities. However, transportation costs for bringing Grand Canyon ore to smelters in other parts of the Arizona Territory would eat into any profits derived from the mines. Passenger revenues could not even begin to cover the costs of operating the railroad. Further, Ripley continued to undercut bonds used to purchase materials from the Santa Fe Pacific, and investors never received any interest. To top it all off, the realization finally struck home that there wasn't enough ore in the area to make a profit on such a large investment.

The last straws began to fall in August 1900. Several mechanics and merchants liens were filed against the railroad. R. R. Coleman, one of the contractors, filed the largest claim, for $28,435.48 in wages owed his workmen (at $1.75 to $2 per day), and another $30,000 for supplies and materials. With no cash to pay off the liens and the outstanding bonds held by other creditors, only one thing could be done. On September 5, 1900, the company went into receivership. The reorganization committee held title to the properties of the railroad until August 15, 1901. Interestingly, several members of this committee—Judge Edward D. Kenna, Byron L. Smith, and James H. Eckels—all served as board members or worked for the Santa Fe.

The Santa Fe Pacific held the largest amount of bonds, totaling $324,000. In addition, they had advanced $200,000 to the reorganization committee for the purchase of the road, to settle claims, and to complete construction of the railroad; $150,000 of this went to pay off the small investors. But this amount didn't even begin to cover the losses of the individuals who had put their businesses and private fortunes at stake for the grand venture. The smaller investors of Williams lost about 90 percent of their original investment. For what amounted to a highly discounted $324,000 in bonds and a $200,000 cash outlay, the Santa Fe Pacific Railroad, under its parent company, the Atchison, Topeka and Santa Fe, became the owner of a nearly completed railroad from Williams to the Grand Canyon.

Final sale on July 20, 1901, and title transfer on August 15 completed the transaction. Complete financial control of the new railroad came with the transfer of 12,053 shares of capital stock to the reorganization committee between September 19, 1901, and March 1, 1902. Lowry Goode assisted the Santa Fe in the liquidation of privately held shares in the Santa Fe and Grand Canyon Railroad until 1911. In correspondence, he repeatedly referred to the Grand Canyon line as "our little road" and commented how close he held it in his heart.

In reality, one wonders what affection he actually held for the line. Goode had his fingers in so many corporations it must have been hard to keep track of them all. In addition to the Grand Canyon line, he was president of two other railroads no longer with us today. The Cairo and Norfolk and the Cairo and Tennessee River Railroad Companies disappeared into history much the same way as the Santa Fe and Grand Canyon did.

On August 10, 1901, the Santa Fe incorporated the Grand Canyon Railway Company in the territory of Arizona. In April 1902, the company went public with issues of capital stock valued at $1,455,000 and paying 5 percent interest. Shares of preferred stock amounting to $250,000 and $1,205,000 in common stock went on the market at $100 per share.

Passenger operations continued while the line was in receivership and after the sale was complete and the company went public. As best as can be determined, the same schedule was maintained with little or no interruption of service.

Times were tough. People were tough. The Grand Canyon Railway might be down but it wasn't out. Its history had now started for the second time.

Unissued Grand Canyon Railway Company
preferred stock certificate No. 50.

Ladder to the Sometime Mine in the Grand Canyon.

THE MINES

N O LESS THAN THIRTY-ONE MINING companies were incorporated in Coconino County between the years 1891 (when it became independent from Yavapai County) and 1904. The number of separate mining claims is astronomical. A great many of these are in the Francis or Grand Canyon Mining Districts, adjacent to the Grand Canyon Railway. Some of these claims and corporations provided justification for the railroad, and others used the railroad, once it became established, to haul ore. Most were not worth the time and effort taken to record them, and many were out-and-out investment scams.

In the Arizona Territory during the 1880s and 1890s, mining was a prime draw for investment and promotion. Miners and promoters recorded claims all over the territory, from north to south and east to west. Companies formed anywhere promoters thought they could raise money for their scams, and not necessarily just in Arizona. Grand Canyon was no different. An article in the distant *Tombstone Weekly Prospector* on October

23, 1890, listed the Grand Canyon Mining Company as having inaugurated business in San Diego "to prospect the Grand Canyon of the Colorado for gold, between Lee's Ferry and the Virgin River."

Hundreds of prospectors poked around anyplace active work had not begun. Some of these prospectors held prominent positions in the territory. Buckey O'Neill and his friends combed the region for signs of "color," becoming more and more convinced money could be made there. O'Neill prospected and staked his claims in the Francis District as one of its more active investors. But he knew as well as anyone else that ore is worthless if it can't be taken out of the ground, transported, and processed at a reasonable cost.

Wagons did not provide an answer to the problem, but a railroad certainly did. But building a rail line to the claims required money—more money than was available in the territory. Several years passed before O'Neill and other prospectors had an answer to this dilemma.

It's important to understand the terrain and geology of the area to comprehend why prospectors and engineers believed the Francis District held great riches, and also to understand why those riches could only provide limited returns for the effort expended. Starting at Williams, at an elevation of 6,700 feet, and moving north along the railroad, the terrain is rolling, with shallow stream cuts. Much of the area forms the drainage for Cataract Creek, which flows through the Havasupai Indian Reservation and into the Colorado River. The surface is dotted with volcanic cinder cones that provided ballast for the roadbed in later years. Vegetation ranges from a variety of grasses grading into juniper, piñon, and denser ponderosa pine. Just north of Williams, the railroad climbs out of town through a beautiful stand of tall ponderosa pines and grades into a piñon-juniper forest after milepost 4, among rolling hills and valleys.

North of milepost 19, the terrain becomes primarily high desert. The profile is one of low rolling hills and wide plains that drop to a low point of 5,800 feet. The vegetation ranges from many varieties of grasses to cliffrose, chamiza, and big sagebrush, then varying densities of juniper and piñon pine.

As you climb up the grade north of milepost 45, outcrops of limestone become readily apparent. Off to the east, Red Butte is visible in the distance with its remnant Moenkopi Formation capped by basalts. At one time, Moenkopi Sandstone as thick as Red Butte is high covered the entire area visible from the railway. Almost all of this material has since eroded away. Remnant Moenkopi is quite apparent in the reddish soils of the region. Vegetation becomes denser as you approach the canyon. Grasses of several varieties and brush grade into piñon-juniper and the denser stands of tall ponderosa north of milepost 51.

There are no great vegetation changes in the dips and rises of Coconino Wash before you reach the South Rim of the Grand Canyon, at 6,800 feet. Here, scrub oak makes an appearance. At the rim, a drop-off of 5,000 feet, ending at the Colorado River, provides a cross section of the terrain you've covered as you traveled from Williams, revealing sedimentary layers of different materials and origins. Episodes of deposition and erosion of marine and windblown sediments left a layer-cake effect. The upper layers of this cake provide the setting for most of the mines of this area, mines that brought the railroad to this region.

Small, scattered copper deposits appear in the strata of the Grand Canyon Mining District. They are found in the breccia (pronounced "breshia") pipes of the South Rim and in the areas south to about milepost 37.

Sorting copper ore for loading onto burros. Some miners transported ore to the railroad in this manner.

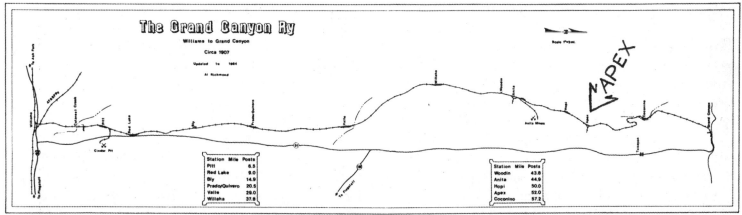

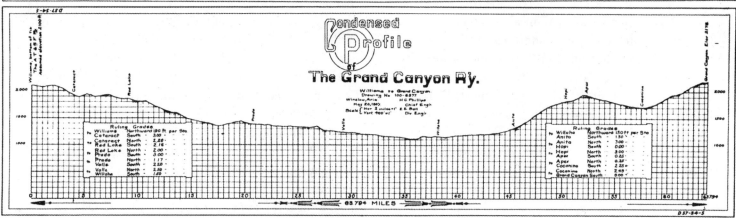

Grand Canyon Railway plan and profile drawings.

Breccia pipes are mostly cylindrical structures composed of angular and frequently rounded rock fragments enclosed in a matrix of comminuted rock paste or subsequently introduced material. In short, they are vertical or horizontal tubes in the host rock filled with material that originated at another location.

The breccia pipes on the South Rim extend through the uppermost layers, known as Kaibab Limestone, the Toroweap Formation, Coconino Sandstone, and Hermit Shale. In the Anita mines area, it is not known if the pipes extend below the Toroweap Formation, as they have not been probed any deeper.

Several theories have been advanced on the origin of breccia pipes in this area. At the rim, it is thought a cavern collapse took place whereby the roof of a cavern, formed when the underlying limestone was dissolved by surface water, collapsed and the cavern was filled in with overlying sediments. In the Anita mines area, the story appears to be different. Present thinking is that the removal of limestone and carbonate cements by rising, reactive hydrothermal (hot liquid) solutions disintegrated the overlying rock layers and generated the collapse. When these hydrothermal solutions flowed into the sediments within the pipes, they transported and deposited minerals that could be mined centuries later.

Whatever the deposition method, the result is highly concentrated ore bodies that are usually very limited in content. Concentrations of copper ore are so high in some of these breccias that they were measured at 65 percent in the early 1900s. Five percent ore is considered very good, so just imagine what riches the prospectors expected from these mines. Many copper mines in Arizona made their fortunes on ore with 5 percent or less copper concentration.

The deepest shaft at the primary Anita claim was only 530 feet before the veins of copper pinched out. And yet this claim provided what might well be the richest assay of copper ore in Arizona history. The deepest and most productive mine in the Francis District was the Orphan Mine on the South Rim of the canyon. A cable tramway ran down the canyon wall to the Supai Formation, where a horizontal tunnel into the breccia pipe provided the means of removing the ore to the surface. When the tramway became hard to maintain, the company updated the mine, digging a 1,600-foot-deep vertical shaft to a 1,400-foot crosscut. The headframe for the mine still stands on the rim to the west of Powell Memorial.

Situated on the rim of the canyon, the Orphan Mine had by far the most diverse mineral content of the mines in the district. Originally a copper claim, it closed down in 1969 after mining uranium, its most profitable ore. Copper showed up in many forms, but the uranium was of the U308 variety. Other ores mined profitably were antimony, barite, cobalt, calcite, gold, iron, lead, molybdenum, silver, and zinc. All in all, a total of thirty-three different minerals existed in the Orphan claim.

At the Anita and Copper Queen mines to the south, the findings were a bit more conservative. Their ores were primarily copper, with dolomite, germanium, goethite, gold, hematite, silver, and U308 in trace or unprofitable amounts. Uranium was found in only a few of the claims. To exploit these resources in the early 1900s, miners used every conceivable method to extract them, with the possible exception of hydraulic mining. Some miners commonly practiced "high-grading" in the claims where small, rich concentrations were found. This process required breaking cobbles by hand with a hammer on an anvil. A piece of railroad track was the usual anvil in this district. Because of the amount of work involved, high-grading is a most unprofitable means of mining, but it became a routine technique in the region during the Depression years. Other methods included using a pick and shovel in near-surface stopes or bulldozers to break up the material for loading.

An asbestos mine deep in the canyon on the north side of the river had to be mined using hand tools. John Hance and his men ferried the ore across the Colorado, transported it to the South Rim by burro, and then loaded it into hopper cars on the railroad. This mine produced some of the longest asbestos fibers known, in excess of four inches. The standard today is around one quarter inch. Hance Mine fibers found their way into theaters around the world in fireproof curtains.

As the word spread in the early 1890s about the rich copper ore in the Francis District, prospectors, promoters, speculators, and flimflam men flooded the area. Mining companies formed overnight with nothing more to show than an address. They all found out one thing: no money could be made without a way to get the ore to a smelter cheaply. Miners were forced to pack the ore out on burros or mules, or to haul it in wagons to a pick-up point on the main line of the Atlantic and Pacific Railway (or later on, the Atchison, Topeka and Santa Fe). Shipping costs quickly wiped out any profits.

After Buckey O'Neill finally convinced Thomas Lombard of the fortunes to be made by building a railroad from Williams to what became Anita, the claims had to be surveyed and consolidated. For this task, O'Neill chose the man who earned a reputation as the most qualified and skilled surveyor in the region: William Lockridge. Having surveyed much of the northern Arizona Territory, he became very familiar with the Francis District and had filed some claims of his own. Even with the relatively unsophisticated instruments available at the time, Lockridge did such thorough work that his surveys have not been improved upon and are still on file at the Coconino County Recorder's Office.

Lockridge also picked up some abandoned claims after the Santa Fe and Grand Canyon Railroad went out of business. He and O'Neill, and later H. K. MacDonald of Williams (originally from Chicago), filed most of the claims for Lombard, Goode and Company. Most of these were incorporated into the Anita Consolidated Copper Company on November 23, 1899.

A majority of the claims represent original filings, but many others had been purchased from miners who did not have enough money to work their claims. Even after the railroad declared bankruptcy, active acquisition and working of these claims continued until 1905, when the Anita Consolidated Copper Company finally abandoned any hopes of large-scale mining in the region. Mining after this time was reduced to

Mine tunnel opening at the Anita claims.

Remains of the ore-loading ramp at Anita constructed by the Atchison, Topeka and Santa Fe Railway for William Lockridge.

small-scale operations, although some of the original Anita claims were explored in the 1980s (and continue to be explored to this day) with the hopes of finding sizeable uranium deposits.

Nuclear fuel companies are presently engaged in uranium mining on the North Rim of the canyon, with extensive exploration taking place on the South Rim. A mining company is fighting environmentalists, the Havasupai Tribe, and concerned citizens over such a mine. Their plan is to establish a large-scale operation east of the old Anita claims a few miles to the east of State Road 64 and only six miles from the South Rim of the Grand Canyon. In April 2015, a U.S. District Court judge denied a request to halt the operation.

This mine is located on the headwaters of Red Horse Wash, which flows directly into Cataract Creek through the Havasupai Indian Reservation and into the Colo-rado River. If one doubts that Mother Nature has the upper hand in this region, consider that a single thunderstorm in 1916 on these same drainages destroyed three bridges, wrecked a train, and killed a fireman. A radioactive pollution disaster can't be ruled out here, just as it wasn't on the Rio Puerco, Little Colorado River, and Colorado River in 1979 when a waste pond dam at the Church Rock uranium mill in New Mexico failed after a thunderstorm. The effects of that disaster will be felt for many generations.

With the railroad in operation, the Anita Consolidated Copper Company built a smelter in Williams at the east end of town in anticipation of the riches believed to be forthcoming from the Anita and Grand Canyon mines. The *Williams News* frequently mentioned the smelter's test runs, and it finally became operational sometime in late 1901 or early 1902. Unfortunately, operating the smelter was an exercise in futility. Because of water shortages under highly suspect circumstances, it never reached full production.

After the collapse of the Santa Fe and Grand Canyon Railroad, the Anita Consolidated Copper Company remained in business and tried to make up for the losses it would sustain with the railroad's failure. The company tried the new "George process," named after its inventor, and made additional test runs. But not enough ore existed to make continued operations profitable in Williams. With the minimal amounts of ore available from the Anita mines, transportation costs on the railroad became prohibitive. For all practical purposes, as long as the smelter remained in Williams it never became operational, although it had the capability of processing ore.

The *Williams News* duly reported the mining news and the hopes and despair of the times. On December 26, 1903, a long editorial on the lack of work in the Francis Mining District told of the plight faced by local miners. "Most claim holders do not have the money to work the claims. They are just holding on waiting for someone else to strike it big and bring them a good price for their claim," the story said.

A major article on February 6, 1904, gave a more hopeful outlook. The story promised expansion of the Anita Consolidated Copper Company, with expectations that a 300-foot shaft would reach 1,000 feet. In evidence of this expansion, the story further mentioned the "smelter, boilers and engine sent to [the] mine to furnish power." The writer boosted the outlook for future prosperity in the Francis District with a notation: "Hance Asbestos Company to begin on a large scale and Canyon Copper Company will also increase."

An even longer article the following week, on February 13, noted, "The smelter in Williams has been shut down...the ore was not rich enough to pay for transportation and smelter charges." Who or what was to be believed in these conflicting stories? Prospectors and miners are eternal optimists, but stories such as these must have kept the people of the Francis District in a quandary.

Such news did not totally dismay the miners at Anita, however. If Muhammad could not go to the mountain profitably, then they would bring the mountain to Muhammad. An article in the May 14 issue of the *Williams News* stated, "Materials [boilers and firebrick] from the Williams smelter was loaded in cars ready to go to Anita." Remnants of the firebrick and slag can still

Lockridge cabin, built in 1905 at the Emerald Mine, one of the original Anita claims.

be found at Anita today. The smelter must have been packed up and sent on very short notice, as an article in the *Boston Globe* dated June 4 commented on a trip made by a Colonel J. T. Small of Lewiston, Maine. It described the area as

a region rich in mineral deposits that may be mined at a small outlay on account of the formations so near the surface. The most promising properties in that wealthy district, in my opinion, after an examination covering 12 days, are the claims of the Anita Copper Company. These mines are located 15 miles south of the rim of the grand canyon [*sic*] on the new tourist railroad to the canyon, the Santa Fe and Grand Canyon branch of the Santa Fe railroad. The railroad runs right to the mine and from there south 47 miles to Williams, where the company's smelter is located.

As the article stated, Colonel Small had just returned from Arizona on June 2, and it is interesting to consider that his train must have been leaving Williams just about the time the Anita Consolidated Copper Company packed up its smelter. If he truly made an independent survey, he must have been given a very selective tour and not allowed to read the local papers, as he further stated in his article:

On the 33 Anita claims most of the work has been done in open cuts so you can see the rich strata near the surface. The cuts run from 15 to 40 feet deep. They have one shaft in the North Star mine that is down to 300 feet, and they propose to continue sinking this shaft and to run drifts from the same. I was amazed at the ore I picked up. I found that the ore runs from 8 to 40 percent copper, and in many instances assays as high as 60 percent.

The Anita mines are most advantageously located with their 700 acres right on the railroad. Ore is loaded on cars at the mine and delivered at the company's smelter at Williams. The smelter is a first class plant, and the company owns 160 acres at Williams. On the whole I never saw any mining proposition that seems to have such great possibilities as the Anita.

One must wonder at the qualifications of Colonel Small to make such a survey. Possibly he was a shill for the company in its attempts to secure additional eastern funding for the project, or the failing company was merely using him. These thoughts come to mind because of his reference to the "Santa Fe and Grand Canyon branch." Since 1901, the line had been the Grand

Canyon Railway. Lowry Goode was the president of the Santa Fe and Grand Canyon Railroad when it failed, and at the time of the article, he was president of the Anita Consolidated Copper Company. He continued for many years to refer to that line as his "little line," and it would be easy to believe his influence on Colonel Small could have produced this story. If he had that much influence, it's not hard to believe Small actually worked for Goode and spoke as directed.

Things went reasonably well for a short period of time, for in the *Williams News* issued November 26, the following notation appeared: "The Anita mine is down to 540 feet in hard sandstone." However, this is as deep as the mine would get. On May 18, 1905, the newspaper reported that work at the Anita Consolidated Copper Company had stopped and all men had been laid off pending settlement of attachment proceedings.

It was all over.

Although large-scale mining of the Anita claims had come to a halt, the effects and evidence of their existence have been apparent for a long time. You can still see the scars upon the landscape, and if you take the time to look through the mining records of the Coconino County Recorder, you'll find all of the names of the claims.

If the romance of mining ever existed, it is expressed there. Hope of good things to come likely inspired the names for the Champion, Lucky Run, and Buster claims. Family, friends, and business associates were immortalized in the Anita, Ethel, Ruby, Richmond, and the Highland Mary. Location determined the names for the Copper Hill, Hillside, North End, Cold Spring, and Log Cabin claims. Possibly the best names, however, came from a miner's fancy: the Copper Prince and Copper

Headquarters shack for the Copper Queen claim, which was south of the Anita claims.

Families who lived at Anita built a fine small community of houses and a school. The owners of this house moved it to Williams when they could no longer make a living at Anita.

Queen, Afterthought, Magician, Wizard, Commodore Dewey, North Star, Willow, Golden Eagle, Hockataia, and the Grand View. Many of these names probably originated in the fuzzy mind of a prospector on a drunken toot celebrating a happy find or in the nostalgic remembrance of friends and relatives back home.

Soon after the hopefully named Copper Queen claim was filed, it came as a pleasant surprise to paleontological scholars of the world when Dr. B. C. Bickell of the Smithsonian's National Museum made an important mammal fossil find there. A subsequent visit in 1904 by Doctor Barnum Brown, also of the National Museum, produced even more fossils.

Miners too discovered the fossils in the Kaibab

Limestone. A deposit of sand seven or eight feet thick, which millions of years ago lay at the bottom of a cave or fissure, buried and helped preserve the fossil remains. As the Kaibab is of marine origin, these fossils of terrestrial mammals are a unique and significant find that included eight previously unknown species. The site could have been a depression with water that trapped the animals as they came to drink. Animal remains taken from the site include badger, camel, rabbit, woodchuck, packrat, pocket gopher, wolf, pronghorn, peccary and squirrel. Although broken up, the bones remained in a good state of preservation. All of these specimens are still part of the National Museum of Natural History's collection in Washington, D.C. Not a bad haul for an "unprofitable" claim.

But romance of the claims names and paleontological treasures found there didn't extend to the hard work required to wrestle meager sums from tons of rock. Miners spent many hours digging in a damp hole in the ground. Many songs have been written about their work and its dangers. And memories of the community they built remain as well.

Anita consisted of about twenty families. There was a section with a bunkhouse for the railroad workers and a livestock shipping point for the ranchers. The mines used the ramp located by the stockyards to load their ore into railroad cars. A small school district was established and children were taught in a converted boxcar, opened around 1920. Later, it grew into a nice schoolhouse, complete with a small bell tower. In 1928 it burned down, and another boxcar replaced it in 1929. The school remained open into the early 1940s.

Residents built several nice houses and a small store with a post office. Bill Lockridge's wife, Grace, served as postmaster from August 1914 until it closed in August 1918. The Anita-Moqui District Forest Service Station was headquartered here prior to being relocated to Tusayan. None of these buildings remain at Anita; some were moved to Williams in the 1950s, and the rest were dismantled.

On April 23, 1969, the last ore train, loaded with uranium from the Orphan Mine and bound for New Mexico, left the siding at milepost 63 behind locomotives 735, 1339, and 1317. As engineer N. S. McLean sounded the horn, pushed the throttle forward, and began to pick up speed, one wonders if he gave a thought to the closing of an era. Mining had brought the railroad to the rim of the Grand Canyon, and that purpose no longer existed. As the train drifted down the grade to milepost 45 and what had been Anita Junction, perhaps the conductor, D. G. Jennings, mused over the dreams of the miners in Anita. Certainly it was worth at least a parting thought.

Engine No. 282 with the first passenger train from Williams to the Grand Canyon.

COMPLETION & REBUILDING

I N 1901, THE GRAND CANYON RAILWAY commenced operations legally as a new and separate company, but in reality the Atchison, Topeka and Santa Fe retained control. Company president E. P. Ripley and the Santa Fe Board of Directors now had what they wanted: a rail line to the rim of the Grand Canyon. The process of acquisition entailed considerable legal maneuvering, luck, and poor business management on the part of Lombard, Goode and Company over a period of several years, but now the Santa Fe owned the railroad outright.

All of the right-of-ways, sidings, passing track, and spurs were theirs, amounting to 63.81 miles of main line, with 53.62 miles in service and the remainder yet to be built; 13.232 miles of yard tracks and sidings; and 2.87 miles of spur track to the Anita mines. In reality, the Atchison, Topeka and Santa Fe acquired a second-class road, because the Santa Fe and Grand Canyon people had been in a hurry to build the line and cut a few too many corners.

The inherited roadbed could hardly be considered anything more than a logging dirt track, with ties laid on the grade without ballast in many places and dirt ballast on the rest. Before operations could continue safely, the new Grand Canyon Railway Company began improvements, classifying them as "additions and betterments." Projects such as widening embankments, ballasting the entire line, and building passing tracks (sidings) received the highest priorities. Ripley planned for the construction of hotels, curio shops, depots, and other facilities, but these projects were put on hold until the completion of the right-of-way construction. Other facilities included the section houses and bunkhouses, and water towers and cisterns at the stations along the line. Much work needed to be done.

Completion of the main line to the South Rim of the Grand Canyon topped the list of Santa Fe priorities. With the railroad in place, the company could begin to develop the area and make a return on its investment. Anticipation in Williams ran high, as an item in the July 13, 1901, issue of the *Williams News* indicated: "[Santa Fe contractor] B. Lantry & Sons, so it is rumored, will complete the canyon railroad shortly almost in the twinkling of an eye." A story in the July 27 issue clearly showed they wasted no time. "Work is progressing rapidly on the completion of the Grand Canyon Railway. Over one hundred teams and all the men possible to secure are working for B. Lantry & Sons of Strong City, Kansas, who are rushing the work to completion as fast as possible."

Another article in the September 14 edition gave testimony that Lantry's crews had lived up to their press. "On Wednesday [September 11] of this week the laying of steel was finished. Ballasting and putting in the necessary 'Y' at the terminal yet remains to be done. The first train is due to be run by next Tuesday [September 17]." And it did, for the issue of September 21 gave the following account:

The first regular train to cover the entire distance from Williams to the Grand Canyon made the trip on last Tuesday. The roadbed is in first class condition and a good rate of speed is maintained the entire length of the line. The schedule was: Williams to the Grand Canyon at 7:00PM-10:00PM; Grand Canyon to Williams at 8:30AM-11:20AM.

There is disagreement about whether this train made the trip as a passenger or freight train. Subsequent accounts have left confusing evidence for both the date and consist. The classic photo, which appeared in *The Santa Fe Magazine* of December 1929, shows locomotive 282, a ten-wheeler 4-6-0 of the 281 class,

and a consist of three water cars and a combination passenger/baggage car with engineer Harry Schlee at the controls and conductor Less Waddlee in charge. The caption reads, in part: "First train to carry passengers to the Grand Canyon of Arizona. The party shown in this photograph left Williams, Ariz. on September 18, 1901, and took the last stage coach from the end of the railway to the cañon, some eight miles distant."

This same photograph was dated September 20 when it appeared in a 1930 *Coconino Sun* (Flagstaff) story. If this date is correct, it could reasonably mean the passengers stayed overnight on September 19 and returned to Williams the morning of September 20, but this is not likely. Additionally, the list of people in the photograph in the *Sun* story includes at least one individual who could not possibly have been there. Emery Kolb did not arrive at the canyon until October 1902. To compound the situation, other sources quoted as late as 1986 have given the date of this first train as September 16. It would be nice to nail the date down exactly, but records of Santa Fe train movements prior to 1930 are fragmentary at best and in most cases, nonexistent.

So let's give credibility to the newspaper stories printed at the time rather than subsequent articles written at least twenty-eight years later. No evidence exists from 1901 to show the train as a freight consist. Similarly, the *Williams News* stories giving the date of September 17, 1901, for the first scheduled passenger train from Williams to the Grand Canyon is the most logical. The classic photo would have been taken on the morning of September 18, prior to the train's expected 8:30 a.m. departure from Grand Canyon.

Effective with Time Table No. 2 of October 1, 1901

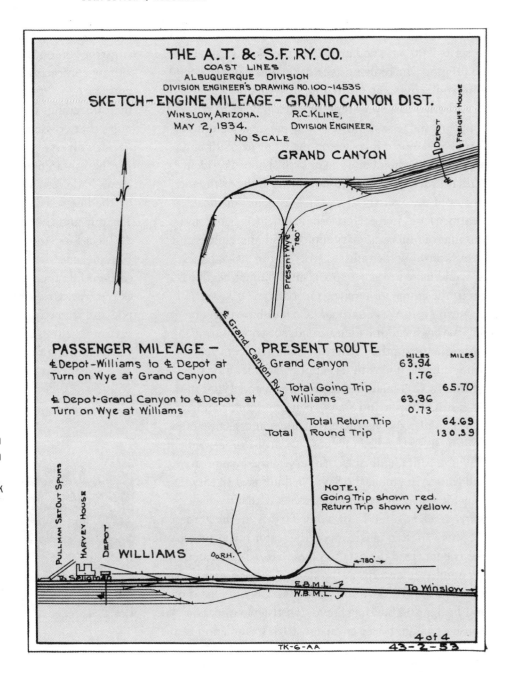

Atchison, Topeka and Santa Fe Railway engineering drawing showing the track from Williams to the Grand Canyon. Yards at both locations are detailed, and the roundhouse location at Williams is also shown. The track north of the roundhouse went to the stock-yards. Many of these tracks and facilities have been retired.

(the first published timetable), train number 10 left Williams at 7:00 p.m. and arrived at the Grand Canyon at 10:00 p.m. The return was by train 11, leaving at 9:00 a.m. and arriving at 11:50 a.m. in Williams.

Although this event represented big news to the people of the region, for the most part, national news stories preempted its place on the front pages of newspapers. On September 6, an anarchist shot President William McKinley. He did not die until the 14th, and stories of the assassination, the president's medical treatment and funeral, governmental succession, and speculation on assassination plots and anarchists ran for weeks, pushing the railroad story to the inside pages. It would have been nice to see some banner headlines about the completion of the railroad.

News from Washington, D.C., had little effect on day-to-day life along the railroad, so work continued without interruption. After the ballasting came consolidating the line with its support facilities along the right-of-way. Sometime between 1899 and 1905, the Atchison, Topeka and Santa Fe and B. Lantry and Sons completed construction of spurs and section crew housing at Pitt (called milepost 6.5 at the time), Valle, Willaha, Anita, and Apex. To service the locomotives and station at Anita, the Santa Fe built two twenty-four-foot-diameter steel water tanks with a twelve-car water track two-tenths of a mile farther up the grade. "Extras" spotted tank cars on the water track, where crews connected the cars to pipes that fed the water, using gravity, to cisterns at the station. Section crews also installed spur tracks at the Hopi and Coconino stations, and bridge and building crews constructed a section house and bunkhouse at milepost 18. Completion of the

right-of-way by the Santa Fe ended nearly two years of construction on the main line. To this end, the railway and its contractor installed and ballasted 270,400 ties with 21,634 fifty-two- or fifty-six-pound relay rails and their fastenings on a roadbed covering nearly sixty-four miles that crossed more than fifty-six bridges and sixty-one culverts.

The Santa Fe and Grand Canyon Railway bridge crews had constructed the longest and highest bridge on the line just north of Valle, over Spring Valley Wash. The pile and frame trestle is reported to have been over 300 feet long and 50 feet high. Around 1918, the Santa Fe replaced it with a 118-foot masonry bridge under earthen fill. Today, the longest bridge on the line crosses Cataract Creek at milepost 4. This 182-foot-long pile and frame trestle spans the headwaters of a stream system reaching all the way to the Colorado River. Culverts along the line are constructed of either metal,

Pile and frame bridge over Cataract Creek at milepost 4. At 182 feet, this is the longest bridge on the Grand Canyon line. The ballast train on the bridge is the first ordered train for the new Grand Canyon Railway.

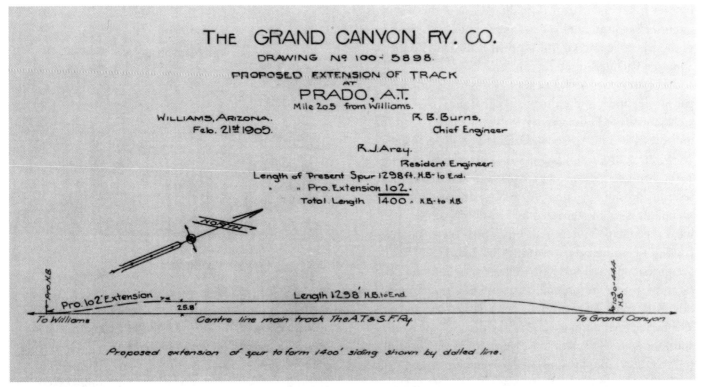

THE GRAND CANYON RY. CO.

DRAWING Nº 100-5898.

PROPOSED EXTENSION OF TRACK
AT
PRADO, A.T.
Mile 20.5 from Williams.

WILLIAMS, ARIZONA.
Feb. 21st 1905.

R. B. Burns,
Chief Engineer

R.J.Arey.
Resident Engineer.

Length of Present Spur 1298 ft. H.B- to End.
" Pro. Extension 102.
Total Length 1400 · H.B- to H.B.

Pro. 102' Extension
25.8'
To Williams
Centre line main track The A.T.& S.F. Ry

Length 1298' H.B. to End.

To Grand Canyon

Proposed extension of spur to form 1400' siding shown by dotted line.

Grand Canyon Railway Company engineering drawing on linen showing the track extension in 1905 at Prado, Arizona Territory (later Quivero).

concrete pipe, or timber. One hundred twelve curves and twenty-seven grade crossings between Williams and the Grand Canyon also require attention and maintenance. For such a short line, there has been plenty to keep the roadmaster, section gangs, and bridge and building crews busy.

In 1905, the Santa Fe renovated and upgraded several of the single-switch spurs to passing tracks (sidings) with turnouts at both ends. With these improvements, longer trains could use the sidings at Red Lake, Prado,

Valle, Willaha, and Hopi to greater advantage. Facilities along the line began to look more complete. The plan view of the railroad now appeared pretty much in its final form, with only a few minor adjustments to be made over the years. Stations along the right-of-way were as follows:

Williams (MILEPOST 0). Southern terminus of the line. Location of a station, telegraph, roundhouse, yards, connection with the east-west main line, section house and gang, and after 1908, a combined Fred

Harvey hotel and station. Combined use of the Williams facilities has been in effect by agreements from the time of the Santa Fe and Grand Canyon Railroad and the Santa Fe Pacific Railroad.

Pitt (MILEPOST 6.5). Location of a section house, gang, telephone, and a thirty-six-car siding (based on eighty-five-foot Pullman cars with allowance for a four-unit diesel and heater unit). Originally built as a spur in 1899, the railroad upgraded Pitt to a passing track in 1905. Prior to 1906, company records referred to the section and siding as milepost 6.5, and the origin of the name Pitt is unknown. It could have been named for local sheepman William Pitt, but it possibly is a corruption of "cinder pit," as one is located there. Use of the pit commenced in 1906 with the reballasting of the Grand Canyon line and construction of a wye at milepost 7, with the spur running east-southeast to the pit. The Santa Fe abandoned use of the pit and retired the spur about 1924. Perrin family descendants, who still own the surrounding land, with ownership dating back to the 1880s, do not remember anyone in the region named Pitt for whom the siding could have been named. Lilo Perrin expressed emphatically that no cattle- or sheep-loading operation existed at Pitt as Byrd Granger's *Arizona Place Names* states. The Santa Fe retired the siding at Pitt in 1942 and abandoned the section on April 1, 1947.

Red Lake (MILEPOST 9). Location of a thirty-one-car siding primarily used for cattle and sheep loading and a telephone. Named for a lake across the highway that takes on reddish hues from Moenkopi silt washed in during rains. The community boasted a post office for a short time in 1888, and a telegraph office operated for

Volcanic cinder cone with cinder pit on the lower right slope, looking northeast from Pitt station at milepost 6.5.

a short period in the early 1900s. Originally built as a spur in 1899, crews extended and upgraded it to a siding in 1905 and to its present size in May 1928. Probably abandoned in 1956, with tracks retired in 1974.

Bly (MILEPOST 14.9). Location of a nine-car spur and a telephone, built for rancher Fletcher D. Bly by the Santa Fe in April 1917. The contract included a concrete water tank and corrals for sheep loading. Retired by the railroad on December 12, 1941, material from the spur was used in construction of the spur at milepost 18. The crossing at this point is a remnant of the Beale Wagon Road.

Milepost 18 (ACTUALLY AT MILEPOST 18.2). Location of a section house, gang, and a telephone. After the sections at Valle and Anita were abolished in 1941 and 1942, the section at milepost 18 became responsible for maintenance of track from milepost 10 to milepost 45.

The Williams section covered milepost 0 to milepost 10, and the Grand Canyon section covered milepost 45 to milepost 63.8. The railroad abolished the section on June 15, 1954. At this time, and until abandonment of the line, the sections at Williams and Grand Canyon split responsibilities for maintenance at milepost 39. The company installed a 610-foot spur in December 1941 and retired it in 1974.

Prado (MILEPOST 20.5). Location of a twenty-three-car siding and a telephone. Originally built in 1899 for cattle and sheep loading by several ranchers. *Prado* is Spanish for "meadow," and this certainly is a pretty meadow. Renamed Quivero in August 1908 because there is a larger station named Prado near Corona, California.

Quivero (MILEPOST 20.5). Supposedly named for Quivera, one of the mythical cities for which Coronado searched in 1540. The reasons for choosing this name and the change of the ending from *a* to *o* are unknown. Originally built as a spur, the railroad rebuilt it as a siding in 1905 and extended it in 1929 and again in 1931 to its present twenty-three-car siding size. Siding track and turnouts were retired in 1974. The Santa Fe built the present loading pens about 1917, rebuilt them in 1936, and in 1974 retired and sold them in place. They are still in use by local cattle and sheep ranches.

Valle (MILEPOST 29). Location of a section house, gang, telephone, and a thirty-seven-car siding for cattle and sheep loading. Originally built as a spur in 1899, the Santa Fe rebuilt it as a siding in 1905 and again extended it in March 1929 to its present size. The name is Spanish for "spring valley." The railroad built the loading chutes for the Grand Canyon Sheep Compa-

ny in 1919. It is presently the headquarters of the Bar Heart Ranch, which purchased all structures in 1941 when the railroad retired them in place. Cattle are still loaded from this location today, but all transportation is handled by truck. This station occasionally appears in the record as Abra, and locals apparently called it Abra Crossing. The name Abra ceased to be used in the 1930s (it is probably an Anglo corruption of *cabra*, the Spanish word for "sheep.") The railroad abolished the section on January 19, 1941, and retired the siding track and turnouts in 1974.

Willaha (MILEPOST 37.8). Location of a section bunkhouse, telephone, and a twenty-four-car siding for loading cattle, sheep, and ore. Named after a Supai Indian word meaning "watering place." Originally built as a spur in 1899, the railroad extended and upgraded it to a siding in 1905. The Santa Fe built the water tank, warehouse, and corrals for the C. L. DeRyder ranch in 1919 and renovated them in 1940. Leases extended to the Azurite Copper Company in 1903 and the Hougue Mining Company in 1907 provided for copper ore loading. The date of section abolishment is unknown, but the Santa Fe retired the siding track and turnouts in 1974.

Woodin (MILEPOST 43.8). Location of a one-car spur for cattle and sheep loading. Upgraded to three-car capacity on December 15, 1937. Originally built by the Santa Fe in 1917 for the Pittman Valley Land and Cattle Company and later leased to the Grand Canyon Sheep Company in 1930, and again in 1937 to the Babbitt Brothers Trading Company. The origin of the name is unknown, but a strong possibility exists that the Santa Fe named it after W. H. Woodin, president of the American Car and Foundry Company, which built railway cars.

Remains of the station at Willaha in 1973 showing buildings, corrals, and siding. The Santa Fe retired the siding and other facilities in 1974.

Remains of Willaha in 1984. Note that the siding has been removed, the station sign is missing, and the buildings have deteriorated. The wooden building to the right is a former Saginaw and Manistee Lumber Company bunkhouse, moved down from Apex in 1936.

The railroad retired the siding track and turnout in 1974.

Anita (MILEPOST 44.9). Location of a section house and gang, telephone, stockyards, U.S. Forest Service headquarters, school, post office, forty-car wye, twelve-car water track, ore loading ramp, the 2.87-mile spur to the Anita mines (retired in September 1917), a 1,250-foot siding (shortened in September 1917 to a four-car spur for the U.S. Forest Service), two water tanks, and a fair-sized community. Named for Anita Lombard and originally called Anita Junction when built in 1899. William Lockridge contracted with the Santa Fe for construction of the ore ramp in 1918. On January 31, 1942, the company abolished the section, and by 1956 all structures had been removed. All that remains today are the ore ramp and the stockyards, originally built by the Santa Fe in 1909, enlarged in 1913, retired in place, sold in 1974, and still in use by the CO Bar Ranch and others. The track was retired in 1942, with the exception of the wye, which they retired in 1972.

Hopi (MILEPOST 50). Location of a twenty-three-car siding and a telephone. Most likely installed as a doubling track for the five-mile-long Anita-Apex grade and later used as a setout for the logging trains from Apex. Named in all probability for the Hopi Indians. Established about 1901 as a spur, and later extended in 1905 and again in 1928, the railroad retired the siding on November 14, 1942, with the removal of the rails, switches, and switch ties.

Apex (MILEPOST 52). Location of a section house, gang, telephone, and a thirty-one-car siding. Originally built as a passing track in 1901. In 1928, it became the location of the Saginaw and Manistee Lumber Company operations, with an eighty-five-car wye and spur.

Railroad track gang in the early 1930s. Gandy brand tools and workers' rhythmic chants to coordinate the alignment of rails are the source of the nickname "gandy dancers."

the northern terminus of the line and transfer point for the Grand Canyon stage while construction by the Santa Fe and Grand Canyon Railroad and later the Atchison, Topeka and Santa Fe moved north to the rim. Used at least part of the time to set out water cars from the Grand Canyon. Named for the wash in which it is located. Retirement of the siding probably occurred in 1954.

Grand Canyon (MILEPOST 63.8). Northern terminus of the railway, with passenger station facilities, telegraph, several tracks used as setouts for trains, a wye for reversing train direction, water tracks for off-loading water into cisterns and tanks, and a section gang. Tracks are numbered from 1 to 41, yet the canyon yards never had forty-one tracks at any one time. (The Santa Fe relocated, renumbered, or combined several tracks over the years.) Additionally, tracks bore names related to their function. Track names such as Old Flume, Garbage, Oil, Gasoline, Barn, Engine, Engine Storage, House, and Powerhouse Spur all saw use from time to time. In 1950, engineering drawings placed the car capacity for the yards at 226, with the stem of the wye able to hold a sixteen-car passenger train with a four-unit freight diesel and heater unit. The section house and bunkhouses were located along the stem of the wye on the east side. Abolishment of the section occurred on May 26, 1969, and from this time on the Williams section handled any necessary maintenance of the line. The tracks were retired between June 13 and 20, 1974, with removal of tracks 3, 4, 17, 21, 23, 27, 29, 33, 35, and 37.

On March 15, 1926, the Williams field engineer conducted a survey for a proposed 600-foot spur at milepost 48 + 1,686 feet. No reason for this spur is apparent, nor

An additional siding held twenty-seven cars. The Santa Fe built these facilities for the lumber company. Apex has been called the high point of the line. Actually, the Grand Canyon rim is higher, but Apex is at the top of the longest and steepest grade, which is where the name probably originated. On June 1, 1930, the Santa Fe abolished the section, and it retired the wye and interchange track in 1942, with removal of the rails, switches, and ties. The siding remained in service until retired in 1954.

Coconino (MILEPOST 57.2). Location of a thirty-four-car siding built in 1900 as a passing track with a telephone. In 1916, a rancher named Henderson contracted with the railroad for the construction of a concrete box water tank for his cattle. Coconino served temporarily as

Track and bridge building gangs rebuilding the roadbed and bridges at Miller Wash after the wreck of July 29, 1916.

is there evidence of it having been built.

In June 1959, at milepost 63, within the national park, the Santa Fe built an ore loading ramp and siding for the Western Gold and Uranium Corporation. This facility serviced the Orphan Mine on the South Rim of the park, and the company loaded ore at this location until April 23, 1969. Retirement of the ramp and tracks occurred in 1974, concurrent with the yard retirements.

A telegraph/telephone line is located on the right-of-way to the west of the track. An agreement between the Santa Fe and Grand Canyon Railroad and the Postal Telegraph Company on May 1, 1896, gave them access to this line. On December 3, 1899, the two companies made this arrangement a joint venture for the next twenty-five years. The Grand Canyon Railway continued this partnership when it took over the line. On December 28, 1920, the Western Union Telegraph Company purchased the Postal Telegraph Company, and a new contract effective January 1, 1921, gave Western Union service rights to the canyon.

Western Union provided telegraph service to the canyon over these lines from the lobby of El Tovar Hotel until 1933, when it closed the office and turned over telegraph duties to the Santa Fe operator at the station. When Western Union stopped service, the Bell Telephone Company began service along the line and to the canyon.

Signal and communications workers for the Santa Fe maintained the line year-round in all kinds of weather. These important lines provided the primary communications link between the Grand Canyon and the rest of the world. The railroad relied upon them for train orders and section communications. People at the can-yon relied on them for doing their business and general communications. Linemen never considered it unusual to be out in a howling gale or snowstorm looking for a break in the line. Everyone knows lines don't break in nice weather.

For many years, the station telegraph operator occupied one of the most respected positions at the canyon. Without the operator, birthday messages and the telegram giving Aunt Martha the arrival time of her favorite niece would not have been possible. In fact, for many years the efficient and safe functioning of the railroads rested in large measure with the conscientious telegraphers.

Telegraph operators transmitted and received train clearances, work orders, company business messages, and Western Union telegrams and money orders. Their responsibilities included passing train orders to train-men by means of bamboo hoops with the order clipped to them. After the engineer or conductor removed the order from the hoop, he dropped the hoop from the train, leaving the operator to hike up the right-of-way to retrieve it. Passengers on the trains could also send and receive telegrams by this system.

Over the years, telegraphers handled a variety of tasks for the railroad. After the Santa Fe installed the Centralized Traffic Control (CTC) system, the telegraphers became part of the main line traffic control. With this system in place, their duties expanded to include throwing switches and monitoring the blocks in their district. In the event of an accident, the dispatcher sent a telegrapher to the site. The operator provided the communication link necessary for safe train movement and transmitted equipment requirements for the crews working to clear wreckage and repair damage. A "brass pounder" held a very responsible and respected position on the railroad.

During World War II, with the labor shortages caused by the war, women became telegraph operators for the first time. Positions such as brass pounder had been male dominated for many years, and it is to the railroad's credit that it began accepting women to fill these very responsible and well-respected roles. Men and women telegraphers worked side by side on the Santa Fe main line and Grand Canyon line for many productive years. With the advent of teletype machines and improved telephone and radio communications, the position of telegrapher faded into the past.

Eventually telephones took over at the canyon, and people along the line began to take advantage of the service too. Several ranches erected their own poles from the main line to the ranch headquarters. Some of these lines extended up to seven miles. It might not have been very convenient for people to travel several miles to make a telephone call at one of the stations, but that certainly beat driving sixty miles to Williams and back over dirt roads. For medical emergencies alone, these lines became worth their weight in gold.

Today the lines are either down or not in service north of milepost 40. Newer lines along the highway service the Grand Canyon. The remaining lines are still in use by ranchers near the right-of-way.

With the advent of the sections, a new way of life came to the region. Section hands, or "gandy dancers," and their families moved into the section houses and bunkhouses. Families with school-age children usually stayed in Williams while the men worked at the section.

Men from Mexico, the territory, and later the state of Arizona filled these positions. In the early 1900s, Chinese and Japanese gangs worked along the line, but they apparently did not take up residence in the sections. The Japanese lived in carbody (boxcar) dormitories located near the roundhouse in Williams. Chinese laborers usually resided in a district on the southeast side of town. This district at one time held the largest Chinese community in Arizona.

Hard work and long days typified life in the sections along the line. Each section usually had four to six men. When the job required tie replacement, every man had a daily quota of fifteen. Men did their own work on ties and didn't help each other unless a new man needed to be taught the tricks of the trade. Tie replacement required a man to pull the spikes, dig out the old tie, pull it out, put a new one in place, spike it to the rail, level it, and tamp ballast around the tie for stabilization. Before the days of machinery, these men did all of this work with hand tools, and each carried his own load and did not depend on others to do his share of the work. As a worker became more experienced, he was able to finish faster and got to take a break until the others caught up with him. The foreman marked ties for replacement when he judged them to be rotted, split, or saw that the tie plates had worn the ties excessively.

Initially the railroads used hardwood ties only on the curves. In later years, the Santa Fe changed many others to hardwood. On this line, ties usually have a life span of twenty to twenty-five years. Normal tie life on heavily traveled main lines is from five to eight years. There are some ties in serviceable condition on this line with date nails from as early as 1923. In 1984, while walking

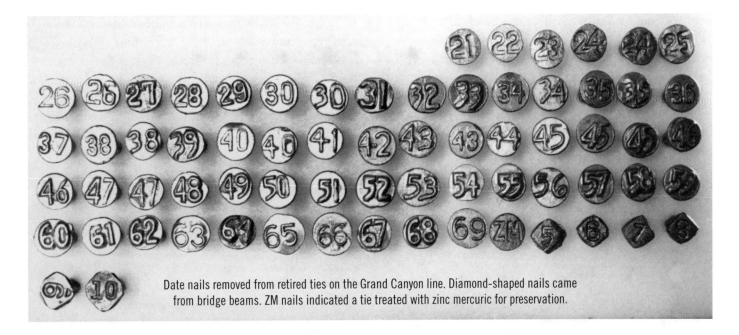

Date nails removed from retired ties on the Grand Canyon line. Diamond-shaped nails came from bridge beams. ZM nails indicated a tie treated with zinc mercuric for preservation.

from the Grand Canyon to Williams along the line, I found one tie in good condition with a 1904 date nail. Talk about preservation!

Daily work schedules for the sections called for eight hours, although during World War II, labor shortages required ten-hour days. Many men left for wartime service or better-paying jobs in defense plants, and this resulted in reduced sections along the Grand Canyon line. Same amount of work with fewer men equals longer days.

In peacetime or in war, railroads require maintenance. Ballast needs to be tamped, ties and rails changed as needed. When the Santa Fe overhauled the line and upgraded the rails from fifty-two- and fifty-six to sixty-five, and later to eighty-five, ninety, and 112-pound rail,

spikes had to be driven, rail anchors set in place, and gauge rods installed to maintain the standard gauge of 4 feet 8½ inches. Rail is designated in pounds per yard. Therefore, a thirty-nine-foot 112-pound rail actually weighs about 1,456 pounds. Consider that, and one begins to get an idea of how hard these men worked. And, over the seventy-six years this railroad was maintained by Santa Fe crews, virtually everything was replaced several times.

Shoddy construction by the original builders caused the Santa Fe to rebuild the line completely, including bridges and culverts, in 1907 and 1908. Upgrading of the rail, although done in different sections at different times, meant each and every rail, spike, and tie plate was replaced a minimum of four times after the original construction. Major overhauls came in 1922, 1924–25, 1927–28, 1930–31, and finally in 1949. Over the years, division engineers ordered several realignments to straighten out curves and take advantage of more-gradual grades.

To maintain standard gauge on the less-stable curves of this line, the crews installed gauge rods at an average of four or five to the rail. Rail anchors are used sparingly along the line, with more in areas near stations and on grades where greater tractive effort is required of the locomotives.

Track work is hard, and it can be dangerous. Accident reports over the years give testimony to broken legs and toes from dropped rails. Fingers were frequently smashed by ties shifting and tools slipping. Lacerations caused by flying steel splinters from mauls or spikes were common. Safety was preached as a religion by the Santa Fe, but accidents always seem to happen.

Probably the worst accident to befall section workers in the course of their jobs occurred on June 29, 1909. An article in the *Williams News* of July 3 reads:

||||||||||||||||||||||||||

Cinder pit operations in 1914 using an oil-fired steam shovel on rails. This method is certainly better than loading the ballast into cars with shovels, as Chinese and Japanese laborers did from 1906 to 1908.

EXPLOSION AT APEX

Three natives of Old Mexico were seriously injured as the result of an explosion of dynamite which occurred at Apex fifty-four miles from Williams on the Grand Canyon railroad, Tuesday. One man was so seriously injured that it is expected he will not recover.

The three men were blasting a rock with several other Mexicans belonging to the same section crew and when a discharge of dynamite did not explode within the regulation time the three went back to learn the cause, an explosion followed with a result as above stated.

The railroad transported all of the injured to the Atchison, Topeka and Santa Fe Railway hospital at Albuquerque, where the one man died of his injuries. Their names never appeared in print.

Construction along the right-of-way required continued use of explosives over the years. To make the line as direct as possible, much of it travels over or through the very hard Kaibab Formation. The only way construction equipment of the day could handle the rock efficiently was to blast it into small fragments. Also, the huge ponderosa pine trees proved to be a barrier to horse teams trying to clear the way. After felling the trees, crews blasted the stumps loose so they could be moved out of the way. The use of explosives could be deadly or even provide some spectacular results, as seen in this story from September 7, 1901:

A peculiar accident occurred near the Bright Angel hotel Wednesday. While the graders were at work clearing the right-of-way, a large blast that had been placed under a mammoth stump, shot the stump into the air until it was a mere speck in the sky. It descended into an unoccupied tent near the hotel, completely demolishing it. It then bounded across the street, tearing up another tent. Fortunately, no one was hurt.

For all of the use of explosives on this line over the years, these two cases are the only known instances of injury or damage.

Standard Santa Fe 21 x 114-foot ten-room concrete bunkhouses provided living quarters for the section crews. The railroad did not provide furniture, so if you brought a bunk you slept on a bunk. If not, you slept on the floor. Each room did come equipped with a wood-burning stove for heat, however. Running water was available if you had a bucket and ran down to the water barrels or cistern. The traditional "little house away from the house" completed the sanitary facilities. Boarding trains also saw use along the line and housed bridge and building crews or supplemental section gangs.

The Santa Fe maintained a store in Williams for its employees and delivered food and dry goods by truck to the sections once a week. The store also stocked tools and work clothes. It only sold the best and most durable items. A man wanted his overalls and gloves to take a lot of abuse and last a long time. Railroad personnel made purchases on credit and had the amount deducted from their salary, but most of the workers and their families did their regular shopping in Williams or at the Grand Canyon, as they considered the company store too expensive.

Entertainment was limited to watching jackrabbits or going to a rare social evening and dance at one of the section houses or in Williams.

Families, especially those with children, usually lived in Williams. Children attended the Mexican school there. In later years, if children lived at the section they attended the one-room schoolhouses at Anita and Apex.

When the section hands joined the service or left to take higher paying jobs, the railroad felt their absence. At this time, the Santa Fe began to hire American Indians, and in doing so created considerable problems in the field. Supervisors could not speak their languages, and the Indians had no knowledge of the work required or the safety aspects of the job. It would not be at all unusual for an Indian, hard at work, to have a train bearing down on him and not be aware of it. The foreman found it difficult to warn crew members of impending danger or even to instruct them in the correct procedures. Also, the Indians were not used to working with schedules and quotas, safety rules and regulations. The situation required much adjustment on both sides in a short time. Indians today comprise a large proportion of the Santa Fe's maintenance-of-way workforce, and many are foremen.

In these years of completion and rebuilding, one instance of legal difficulty came about. In 1906, the railroad needed new ballast. It cost money and time to haul cinders from the cinder pit near Flagstaff. This region is of volcanic origin, and there are cinder cones all along the line. The cone near milepost 6.5 on the Perrin ranch provided the best source of cinders and was easy to access.

As was usual with the railroads of the time, the Santa Fe considered something they wanted as theirs. This situation proved no exception. The railroad needed ballast, and this conveniently located cinder cone had great quantities of it. The Santa Fe filed suit in federal court in Prescott for condemnation by judicial action, also known as eminent domain. Dr. E. B. Perrin was not a lightweight, but the power of the Santa Fe totally outclassed him. The court awarded the cinder cone outright to the railroad.

The Santa Fe wasted no time in building a spur with a wye at milepost 7 to reach the pit. During the original rebuilding and reballasting of 1907–08, Chinese laborers using shovels loaded cinders in gondola cars. They unloaded the ballast along the line in the same fashion. Up until 1924, this pit provided the ballast for rebuilding the Grand Canyon line and for day-to-day needs. Although still owned by the Santa Fe Pacific Corporation, the cinder pit is no longer in service for the railroad. The State of Arizona leases the pit for its cinder needs for area roads.

During these years, the Santa Fe completed all of the major changes along the line. However, much work remained to be accomplished at either end. In August 1901, Williams got a new freight house. To restore some of Williams's prominence as a railroad center, the railroad also built a new six-stall roundhouse with a turntable. This replaced the eight-stall roundhouse moved from Williams to Seligman by the Santa Fe Pacific in 1897. Up until that time, Williams had been a division headquarters. As the range and speed of locomotives increased, the division headquarters moved to Seligman. But with the arrival of the Grand Canyon line, Williams moved back into prominence. The locomotives for the main line and Grand Canyon Railway jointly used these facilities.

Over the years to come, the daily work of maintaining what had been so laboriously built became routine. Only minor changes needed to be made in the alignment of tracks and the changeouts, as noted above. As demands for labor increased on the main line, workforces decrease on the branch lines such as the Grand Canyon Railway's. The Santa Fe reduced sections until only those at the Grand Canyon and Williams remained.

During this period, two corporate moves occurred to merge the Grand Canyon Railway with the Atchison, Topeka and Santa Fe Railway. The first action reduced administrative problems between the two companies. The Grand Canyon Railway had no rolling stock or power of its own and had been required to lease them and all other equipment from the Atchison, Topeka and Santa Fe. Other legal arrangements added to the pile of unnecessary paperwork, so the second action alleviated this by having the Atchison Topeka and Santa Fe lease the Grand Canyon Railway. With this move came the formal listing of the Grand Canyon District of the Albuquerque Division of the Coast Lines in the timetable of March 15, 1925.

Later, in 1942, the Grand Canyon Railway Company formally ceased to exist. On December 31 of that year, the Records of Incorporation of the State of Arizona show the Grand Canyon Railway being reconveyed to the Atchison, Topeka and Santa Fe Railway Company.

By the 1950s, the railroad bulldozed all of the section buildings with the exception of Apex to save on taxes. Skeletal remains of the bunkhouse at Apex and rusting trash piles are the only surviving traces bearing testimony to the living conditions and way of life at sections along the line.

The railroad retired most of the facilities between the 1950s and the 1970s. Material from spurs and sidings no longer in use had to be reclaimed for use elsewhere. When steam ceased to be the main motive power in 1953, the Santa Fe retired the water towers at Anita. The community of Anita dwindled as the railroad reduced its facilities. The U.S. Forest Service moved its headquarters to Tusayan, and the families living at Anita relocated. Several families moved their houses with them; some can be seen in Williams today.

Only a few of the Grand Canyon Railway's sidings and trackside structures exist today. The graded beds and a few old, rotting ties are the only reminders of what was once a busy place. Most of the switches are long gone. Former section buildings are merely piles of broken concrete. Residents and workers have moved on, and quiet belies the life that once existed here.

Cattle crossing the right-of-way at milepost 26. They still present a formidable obstacle to trains.

CATTLE & SHEEP

I F YOU BELIEVE THE MANY RANGE WAR stories in books and movies, cattlemen and sheepmen have always been at each other's throats and always will be. Too many of these stories are true, but happily that was not the case for the ranchers along the Grand Canyon Railway line. Witness to this fact is the funeral of one of the longtime cattlemen of the area. Two of his pallbearers were sheepmen.

Long before the Santa Fe and Grand Canyon Railroad came into being, ranchers raised cattle and sheep on the high desert plains of northern Arizona. Ranching and mining comprised the major industries of the region for many years. The railroad surveys of the late 1800s divided the land north and south of the proposed lines into a checkerboard pattern of one-mile-square sections. Alternate sections were deeded to railroads, individuals, or corporations, with the remainder belonging to the Arizona Territory or the United States. The government leased sections for grazing, and this remains the practice today.

Prior to 1900, ranchers in the Williams area shipped cattle and sheep from stockyards along the main line of the Atlantic and Pacific Railroad and its successors, the Santa Fe Pacific and the Atchison, Topeka and Santa Fe. As track moved north from Williams toward the mines at Anita, area ranchers took advantage of the railroad's presence and began to drive their stock to the closest points along the line for loading. This saved them many hours on the dusty trail, herding livestock to Williams. Until the Atchison, Topeka and Santa Fe built more permanent stockyards along the line in the 1910s, the ranchers loaded their livestock at roughly constructed pens and chutes. Ranchers contracted with the railroad to construct these yards along with the necessary spurs, sidings, or wyes.

In this manner, the railroad worked in harmony with the local population. Not only did it build these yards and sidings for the ranchers, it hauled water to them from the wells at Bellemont and Del Rio (later known as Puro) at cost during the dry seasons.

Water always has been and remains at a premium on the Colorado Plateau during much of the year. From April to June and September to November, the climate is extremely dry. During these months, the railroad became the lifeline for the cattle and sheep industry in this region and allowed ranchers to operate throughout the year.

The Santa Fe spotted tank cars, usually of 12,500-gallon capacity, at ranches and sidings along the line. A freight extra to the canyon usually delivered water to the ranches once a week, but when needs at the national park exceeded the supply from Indian Garden, the dispatcher also scheduled water extras. Train and section crews spotted the cars and pinched them into place so they could fill tanks or cisterns. The railroad provided all of this service for a paltry $18 per car. Even when this cost rose to $28 in the 1960s, it continued to be the bargain of the century for the ranchers.

Today, the ranchers are obliged to haul their water from the wells at Williams or Bellemont with their own trucks. Their cost is considerably more than what the railroad charged. Certainly the railroad did not provide this service merely out of the goodness of its heart. Revenues from cattle and sheep shipments balanced the books, although hauling stock never made a lot of money for the railroad. By the 1950s, the Atchison, Topeka and Santa Fe began to extricate itself from the livestock shipping business because the cost of maintaining stock cars began to exceed freight revenues. When the railroad cut back on service, the ranchers simply moved cattle to market by truck. Shipping by truck proved better for the cattle and less costly to the rancher. It also allowed the railroad to slowly and steadily curtail cattle

Stock extra with 2-10-2 3800 class 3925 in the lead pulls into Williams after loading sheep at Quivero.

Double-deck stock car. The Santa Fe used cars of this type along the Grand Canyon line for sheep and calves.

shipments as equipment became unserviceable. However, during these service reductions, the railroad continued to provide water to ranchers along the line at cost.

Cattle and sheep ranchers in this region face several distinct challenges. The water problem is always serious, and grass is also at a premium. These problems necessitate the constant moving of the bands of sheep (usually 2,000 to a band) and limit grazing cattle to no more than eight or ten head to a section. Due to its austere nature, ranchers jokingly call this "60/40 range," which means a cow must have a mouth sixty feet wide and move at forty miles per hour in order to find enough to eat.

In the early days, stockmen shipped sheep back and forth as the seasons changed along the Santa Fe, Prescott and Phoenix Railway or, as it is usually called, the "Peavine," to Wickenburg, Congress, and Williams. About 1915, this system became too costly and herders began to trail the herds all over Arizona, from east to west and north to south. Herds in the Williams area

Sheep crossing the tracks at Valle, taken with a view to the north. A water car is spotted on the siding.

Andres Aragon tends his Romney and Rambouillet sheep at Valle in 1938.

become a major problem. Without the dogs to act as guards, the herders have the almost impossible task of protecting the sheep. The coyotes steal into the bands before dawn and tear up as many lambs or ewes as they can. It's not unusual for them to kill twenty or more at a time.

Early summer brought the shearing season. For many years, these men had to shear from forty to fifty sheep per day without the benefit of power tools. This is difficult, tedious, backbreaking work. At the end of a day, it was all they could do to drag themselves to their bedrolls.

High-quality wool from the sheep raised in the Grand Canyon District was always in demand from the brokers. Wool revenues produced almost as much for the rancher as it did for the railroad, which shipped 50,000 to 60,000 sheep yearly. Until the advent of ship-

usually numbered about 22,000. At one point, around 1930, about eight million sheep grazed the fields and plains of Arizona. It's difficult to imagine this many sheep on the move.

Tending to these bands of sheep involved quite a variety of people. A caporal had charge of three bands, with one herdsman to look after each. A campero tended to the cooking chores for all of the men. Mexicans made up the majority of those who watched over the vast herds of sheep in northern Arizona, with a few white cowboys working here and there. In later years, Basques came onto the scene, and their descendants remain with us today. All of them worked long, hard hours, with workdays lasting from sunup to sundown, and usually longer.

These herders had well-trained dogs working with them, except in the spring. During lambing, the dogs have to be kept away from the ewes. Coyotes then

Campero transportation at Valle in 1939. Reliable burros were the preferred pack animals.

ping by truck, the ranchers and the railroad had a fairly lucrative relationship.

Sheep ranching is a hard way of life. Those who take up herding sheep usually love being outdoors on the range. In the days of the vast sheep herds, the men always had plenty of food, although it tended to be monotonous. Fried mutton, boiled mutton, and mutton stew were staples. It was a prized campero indeed who could make mutton taste different from day to day. Tending sheep was also a lonely occupation. The herder's dogs and burros furnished his only company for days at a time. For the most part, entertainment was strictly at the hand of the individual. Shearing season provided a good excuse for friends and family to gather at a barbecue. Everyone came to these events to relax and enjoy themselves after they had finished the difficult work of shearing. Herders on the trail occasionally found a break from the routine in towns the herds passed by in their continual search for good forage.

Grazing is the only obvious bone of contention between the sheepmen and the cattlemen of the Grand Canyon District, but most have managed to remain good friends over the years, even with the occasional disagreement over grazing practices. However, if you ask about the effect of cattle and sheep on the range, you will get entirely different answers depending on which side of the fence you happen to be on.

Cattlemen will tell you sheep trample the grass into oblivion or crop it off at ground level, and that there are areas that have never reseeded, even after many years of non-use. Sheepmen are quick to point out that cattle have overbrowsed the protein-rich chamiza brush in the area. Even though efforts by responsible ranchers are underway to reestablish this shrub, it is a slow process. The high desert does not heal quickly. Sheepmen will also tell you cattle foul the waterholes so much that sheep will not drink from them. Those who raise both cows and sheep don't say much one way or the other. Even in paradise there are differences, but these people have found a way to live together in spite of them.

Many of their differences come over abuses of the land. If cattle or sheep are allowed to overgraze, the land will suffer. It all boils down to responsible land use with proper management of the available resources. Smart and responsible ranchers know it is to their benefit to keep the livestock moving from one range to another, allowing the land to renew itself. Rotation of cattle to different ranges and the proper animal-to-acre ratio are key tenets of this philosophy. When you look at different ranches, it is not difficult to see which rancher takes care of the land and which does not. The cared-for ranch boasts a good growth of chamiza and grass, while the other has many barren patches and no chamiza. It's easy to blame either the cattle or sheep for overgrazing, but in reality, the mismanagement of the land by the rancher is the real reason for the differences between cattlemen and sheepmen.

Cattle raising in the Grand Canyon region has always been a tenuous business. Even so, ranchers raising cattle have a more static situation than sheepmen. Ranch headquarters usually allow access to most of the ranch with a minimum of difficulty. Before the advent of cars and pickup trucks, cowboys had to spend much time camping out or living in line shacks to get the daily work done. On a ranch of 300,000 acres or more, this became a way of life for several men much of the year.

Perrin cowboys at the Williams stockyard.

There have always been many respectable people and businesses in Williams, but in the early years hardworking cowboys, railroaders, and loggers made up much of the town. They worked hard and played hard. Some form of action could be found on Railroad Avenue much of the day and night. Fights, knifings, and shootings commonly occurred, and yet this activity seldom flowed over into the "better" parts of town. After a Friday night on the town, the cowboys caught the train back to work on Saturday morning.

The railroad took on the part of a comforting friend and neighbor in this vast country. Ranchers, cowboys, and shepherds felt a little closer to civilization just by being able to hear the train or see its lights off in the distance at night. One rancher over by Mount Floyd, which is about thirty miles west of the railroad, used to set his watch by the night train headed back from the canyon. It was comforting to know that if he needed help, it really wasn't so far away. A train could be flagged at any time to transport an injured or ill person to the doctor in Williams. The telephones at the various stations along the way also gave residents a means to call for help in times of trouble.

Especially during bad weather and particularly in the winter when roads and trails became impassable, the railroad provided a link with civilization. The unusually severe winters of 1918–19, 1948–49, and 1967–68 hit northern Arizona very hard. The railroad and trainmen were worth their weight in gold to the ranchers during these times.

Exceptionally heavy snow created severe problems, but the wind aggravated the situation. Deep drifts foiled any movement, and the world all but disappeared when

Today, with more speedy transportation available, cowboys can travel farther and get more done in a shorter span of time. But many a new pickup truck looks twenty years old its first summer in the field because cowboys will try to drive it wherever a horse can go. And just because a cowboy has a better means of transportation doesn't mean the work is less difficult.

For much of the twentieth century, as with their sheepherder counterparts, cowboys were left to their own devices. Their supplies were sent out to the various locations. Although they spent much of their time on the range, occasionally cowboys flagged the Friday night train and headed into Williams for a bit of diversion.

Williams could provide its share of entertainment. In the early 1900s, bars, Chinese restaurants, and houses of ill repute made up the town's primary businesses.

the wind blew the snow into swirling clouds. Ranchers relied on the railroad for provisions. They'd call in to Polson's or Babbitt's stores in Williams and place their orders. Clerks would deliver the groceries to the railroad station, and the trainmen made the deliveries along the line.

Even the cattle benefited from the train. During the winter of 1948–49, a herd needed to be evacuated from Valle to Williams. The rancher had not expected such a severe winter and had planned to winter the herd over. Heavy storms stranded the cattle. Out in the open without food or shelter, the cattle would die. A phone call to the helpful dispatchers of the Santa Fe got extras and section hands rolling to Valle in short order. Under these conditions, a person standing fifty feet away from the tracks at Valle could not even see or hear the train.

Loading cattle in stock cars at Williams for transportation to market. **BELOW:** Perrin cowboys herd cattle on the ranch just north of Williams.

Grand Canyon Railway southbound No. 18 steams through Valle at twilight, trailing six Harriman-style Pullman cars.
||||||||||||||||||||||||||

It took three trains and three days to get the cattle out and down to the shelter of the yards in Williams. In spite of the weather extremes, the supreme effort on the part of the railroad, friends, and neighbors saved this herd.

Major cattle and sheep shipments usually occurred in the fall, with lambs shipped in the spring. Stock extras brought the cars to various sidings and spotted them for the ranch hands to load. Ranchers used volcanic cinders for bedding in each car and loaded the cars as they saw fit. Shipping time usually found twenty to thirty cars spotted at a siding.

After completing the loading, the ranchers took time for get-togethers, picnics, or barbeques. Shipping points were at locations convenient to several ranches, and the occasions provided a good excuse to renew friendships. The wonderful food gave everyone something to talk about for days afterward.

Remains of the cattle-loading chute with the scale frame in the foreground at Willaha in 1984. Red Butte, with its remnant Moenkopi Formation, is in the background.

The railroad served the ranchers in many ways, and the railroaders were considered friends. Even under less-than-desirable circumstances, they always maintained good relations. However, the prevailing law of the land did bring about a difficult situation with respect to livestock accidents.

Before the railroads arrived in Arizona, cattle interests dictated legislation. Because cattlemen were the source of money and power in those days, it's not difficult to understand why the legislature enacted laws to their benefit. With the enactment of the Open Range Law, livestock owners grazed their herds without restriction. In short, cattle and sheep could wander and graze wherever the grass was. If someone didn't want the herds on their property, then they were responsible for fencing them out.

However, as provided in the Open Range Law, fences along rights-of-way are the responsibility of the railroads. Under this law, any livestock struck by a train are also the responsibility of the railroad. When a train killed a cow or sheep, the rancher simply made a claim and the Santa Fe paid fair market value in short order. This was far more than could be expected of other railroads in the West. Most kept ranchers waiting for months to be paid.

Usually the Santa Fe did not want to get in the business of building stock fences. The railroad found it cheaper to pay the ranchers for stock that had been killed. Ordinarily this region is not heavily stocked due to the type of range. However, at times, some ranchers brought in large numbers of stock and felt they needed protection.

When Lilo Perrin brought 1,200 prime cattle to the area between mileposts 15 and 18 in 1948, he struck a deal with the Santa Fe to fence both sides of the right-

Quivero station as it appeared in 1984. View is to the south from the siding.

of-way for two and a half miles. Perrin provided the labor for the erection of the fence, and the Santa Fe provided the material. This arrangement worked out to the mutual satisfaction of both parties. As long as the Santa Fe didn't have to pay for the labor, it was cost effective to protect the 1,200 cattle through the purchase of the material. It's certain the train crews and the maintenance people who had to clean up the locomotives after a collision also appreciated this arrangement.

A few other ranchers along the line also made use of this arrangement from time to time. But for the most part, the Grand Canyon line operated under the rules of the Open Range Law, without fences. Today's Grand Canyon Railway still operates under these rules.

As we have seen, in many ways railroaders and ranchers came to be family. So it was not out of the ordinary when one of the "rails" gave a puppy to a rancher's young daughter. This puppy grew to be a playful dog whose one great vice was to chase junco birds. Every once in a while, the dog would wander far afield during its favorite pastime. On one such occasion, it had made its way several miles from home when the crew of the local spotted it. The engineer stopped the train, called the pup, and placed it in the locomotive. When he reached the ranch farther down the line, he again stopped the train and the crew hand-delivered the dog to its worried owner.

Because the Santa Fe built most of the Grand Canyon facilities and established the South Rim of the national park as it exists today, the people at the canyon and with the railroad had a close relationship over the years. But the railroad also built many facilities along the line for the ranchers and supported their businesses. And so

The Bar Heart Ranch at Valle station in 1984. It appears much the same today. Cattle-loading pens are to the right, and the ranch headquarters are to the left. The crossing is the scene of the accident that took the life of George Barnes.

the people of the ranches along the Grand Canyon line had a personal and close association with the railroad and its people too. Like family, they shared the good times and the bad.

Today these people look back and swap old stories. You still hear about the bull elk that moved into the Bar Heart Ranch and made himself at home. No one bothered to tell him that he wasn't a cow, so he moved in and out of the herds and corrals. This went on for a while until the Arizona Game and Fish Department decided he needed to be moved. It took a bit of effort to get him under control, but they succeeded in loading the elk into a horse trailer and moving him south of Mormon Mountain. Hopefully, he found friends there as good as he'd had at Valle.

The bull elk that came to visit at Valle and decided to stay. No one bothered to tell him that he wasn't a steer, so he moved right in until Arizona Game and Fish rangers came to relocate him.

These stories came to an end on November 1, 1972, the day of the last cattle shipment on the Grand Canyon line. The Santa Fe spotted eleven cars at Anita and another four at Valle. Conductor R. H. Fulton and engineer J. R. Smith hauled this train behind locomotives 3424, 3460, 3352, 3442, 3254, 3411, 3210, and 3390. Twenty-two days before, on October 10, the last sheep shipment left out of Quivero in twenty-five cars. Conductor J. A. Stanley and engineer M. K. Jennings made this haul with locomotives 3410, 3349, 3239, and 3424. Locomotive 3424 had the dubious distinction of being a part of both trains that marked the end of an era.

Anyone present with any sense of nostalgia must have felt some remorse as those trains pulled out for the last time and disappeared over the horizon into history.

BUILDING GRAND CANYON NATIONAL PARK

WHEN THE TRACK OF THE GRAND Canyon Railway reached the South Rim of the Grand Canyon in September 1901, a new chapter began. Its roots had been established long before the Santa Fe and Grand Canyon Railroad went into receivership. From the letters and messages between E. P. Ripley and his subordinates, we know that the Atchison, Topeka and Santa Fe Railway had made plans for construction of facilities at the South Rim as early as 1899. Letters from Buckey O'Neill to Ripley and Board Chairman Aldace Walker on the subject of tourism solidify their intent. But the situation became a waiting game: Waiting for the inevitable financial collapse of the Santa Fe and Grand Canyon Railroad. Waiting, with a few helpful shoves, for what became the wholly owned Atchison, Topeka and Santa Fe Railway operation.

In 1901, Grand Canyon National Park did not exist. The federal government offered limited protection to the region under the auspices of the Grand Canyon Forest Reserve. When Theodore Roosevelt first visited the area in 1903, the canyon, with all of its magnificent natural beauty, so impressed the president that he became determined to set it aside as a public trust. Even with his help, congressional action to establish part of the canyon as a national monument was stalled until 1908. Congress finally established the National Park Service as part of the Department of the Interior in 1916, and in 1919 Grand Canyon finally reached national park status. Between the time the Santa Fe reached the rim and the establishment of the park, the railroad became the driving force that opened up and developed this spectacular place for all to see. For this, and for doing it in a manner that did not detract from the natural wonder itself, the American people owe the Santa Fe a considerable debt of gratitude.

There are those who would disagree, believing the park should have been left completely natural with no signs of human habitation. It's a nice thought, but hardly realistic. Even today, the canyon remains off the beaten track, and had it not been for the railroad, many millions of people might never have seen this wonder. The canyon is as much theirs to see and visit as those who prefer a more primitive scene.

Railroad planners showed restraint and good taste in developing the park without defiling the natural surroundings. They had their work cut out for them. In 1901, the railroad arrived upon a scene bordering on chaos. Tent camps and nondescript hotels cluttered the rim near Bright Angel Trail, with no plan or thought of aesthetics. Over the years, the Santa Fe replaced these camps with the structures that now grace the South Rim. With the engineering skills and technology of the times, the railroad made a wonderful contribution that has allowed generations of Americans and people from around the world to experience Grand Canyon without insulting their sensibilities.

|||||||||||||||||||||

Schoolteachers' special stopped at the original Grand Canyon Depot on the way to the Saint Louis World's Fair in 1904. Engineer "Grizzly" Anderson and fireman Jack "Curley" Lancaster stand beside their doubleheaded 2-8-0 consolidation.

Naturalist John Muir could not find it in himself to complain of the trains and development at the South Rim. When he visited the canyon late in 1902, he wrote:

When I saw those trains crawling along through the pines of the Cocanini [*sic*] Forest and close up to the brink of the chasm at Bright Angel, I was glad to discover that in the presence of such stupendous scenery that they were nothing. The locomotives and trains are mere beetles and caterpillars, and the noise they make is as little disturbing as the hooting of an owl in the lonely woods.

Aerial view of Grand Canyon Village taken about 1935. Part of the yards are visible, along with the new powerhouse, Kolb and Lookout Studios, and Bright Angel Hotel (before renovation—note the tent cabins).
⊔⊔⊔⊔⊔⊔⊔⊔⊔⊔⊔⊔⊔⊔⊔⊔⊔⊔

In truth, most of the railroad lies in a depression behind the rim. The natural stone and wood buildings are also behind sightlines along the rim, and to even notice them one is required to look away from the overpowering beauty and vastness of the canyon. Even when viewed from the air or Maricopa Point, which juts into the canyon, looking east toward the village, the community blends quite well into the rolling terrain of the forests.

A common question arriving passengers asked at the station indicates how well this community blended in with the natural surroundings: "How do you get to the Grand Canyon?" Newly arrived tourists probably drove the station personnel to drink with the frequency of this question. Today, people detraining Grand Canyon Railway cars still ask.

As early as 1892, both crude and elaborate tourist accommodations occupied the rim. Bright Angel Camp handled the hardy few who made their way to the canyon by way of stagecoach or wagon. This tent camp consisted of canvas-covered wooden-framed "cabins"

Tent kitchen for the original Bright Angel Camp about 1900. Note the freshly baked pies on the table.

furnished with cots or beds of dubious comfort. Cooks produced meals in a dirt-floored tent, which functioned as a kitchen, and then served them in a wooden-floored "dining room." Much of the provisions and bedrolls for these guests arrived with them, in a wagon that rode next to or trailed behind the coach. Not first-class, but certainly adequate. As rustic as these facilities might have been, the travelers probably considered them a welcome sight after the rugged ten- to eighteen-hour journey.

By the mid-1880s, several stage and livery companies operated out of Flagstaff, Williams, and Ash Fork. Some provided only transportation to the available facilities on the South Rim, and others ran cabins and hotels they themselves established for the tourist trade. Fernando Nellis operated out of Williams to facilities near Grandview Point owned by "Captain" John Hance and William Hull. This log cabin structure did not offer much in the way of creature comforts, but there was a panoramic view of the canyon and access to the caverns below the point with their crystal and stalactite formations. Hance and Hull also started the first stage service to the canyon from Flagstaff.

William Wallace Bass and Martin Buggeln also ran liveries and coaches and operated tourist accommodations at the rim, in addition to transporting passengers from communities south of the canyon. Bass ran from Williams and later from Ash Fork to the west rim (so called because it is west of the South Rim, or Grand Canyon Village area). Here, for many years, he operated Bass Camp and later Bass Hotel. His camp offered rough living, and visitors to the small wooden hotel did not fare much better. But Bass Camp had as its drawing card the magnificent Supai Canyon (also called Havasu Canyon or Cataract Canyon), a tributary of the Grand Canyon. This is the beautiful home of the Havasupai Indians, with its lush valley, blue waters, travertine pools, and spectacular waterfalls. It is difficult to get to, but Bass had the exclusive use of this route.

Bass later worked out an arrangement with the Atchison, Topeka and Santa Fe for a flag stop at milepost 59. Here passengers detrained and traveled to Bass Camp via stagecoach. They made the return trip by simply flagging down the train at the same location.

Buggeln worked out of Williams, with Grandview Point as his destination. Here he built a comfortable, reasonably modern two-story hotel. As the largest hotel on the rim around the turn-of-the-century, the Grandview provided the finest lodgings at the canyon.

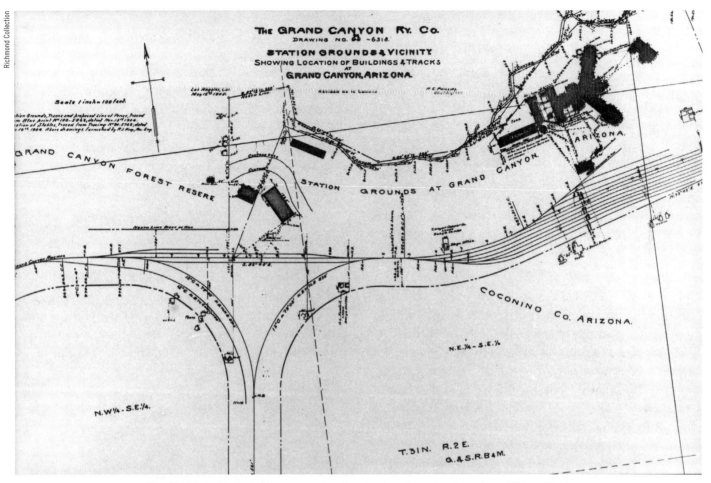

This 1905 Grand Canyon Company engineering drawing shows the wye and new El Tovar Hotel.

The Bright Angel Hotel with Buckey O'Neill's cabin to the right on the South Rim of the Grand Canyon.

the Grand View Hotel.

Buckey O'Neill built his log cabin and bunkhouse late in 1896 on the rim, where the present-day Bright Angel Lodge is now located. It was possibly the first cabin built on the South Rim and is certainly the oldest surviving structure in Grand Canyon Village. The cabin is still part of the Bright Angel complex. O'Neill probably built it for his own use and as a place to entertain friends. He eventually divided it into two rooms and later sold it to Ralph Cameron prior to leaving for his date with destiny in Cuba.

Sanford Rowe bought out the Williams livery business from William Bass in 1892 and spent the next several years supplying South Rim businesspeople with their freight requirements. He staked some mineral claims about three miles west and south of the village and built a small log hotel there. Over the years, it grew into a tourist complex with a hotel, cabins, and an entertainment facility that included a bowling alley. A

Grandview even held the distinction of being the first post office at the rim, under the name of Tourist, with Hance as the postmaster from May 1897 to April 1899. What happened to this post office between 1899 and March 1902 is not clear. When the railroad came to the rim in 1901, Buggeln went to work for the Santa Fe at Grand Canyon and he accepted the position of postmaster there in March 1902. Interestingly enough, the post office at Grandview was reestablished in November 1903, this time with the name Grandview and with Harry Smith as postmaster. Again short lived, it lasted only until November 1908. Both Hance's and Buggeln's hotels have been long since destroyed by the park service in order to restore the area to a more natural site.

Several other enterprising individuals built facilities in the present Grand Canyon Village in the 1890s. Buckey O'Neill built a cabin and bunkhouse, Sanford Rowe established Rowe Well, and the Cameron brothers erected

The Grand View Hotel about 1903, with the original Kolb Studio in the left foreground.

popular spot with the residents of the village, this watering hole provided some relief from the ever-present tourists. Here, they could get away and have a friendly drink, bowl a few games, and enjoy some dancing. By the late 1950s, many of the wooden frame and log buildings had deteriorated to a condition beyond repair. To ensure safety and the aesthetics of the natural scene, the park service demolished them. In April 1961, the park removed the last structures. All that remains today of Rowe Well is a picnic ramada next to the tracks.

The Cameron brothers, Niles and Ralph, were up to their ears in their mining interests and the Bright Angel Trail. These mines never did produce ore sufficiently rich to be worth production, but the claims gave the brothers a good excuse to exercise their right to the trail and charge a toll of one dollar per animal for its use. They spent many years in litigation with the Santa Fe over these rights only to lose. Considering that Ralph Cameron became a territorial representative and later a United States senator, one might begin to understand

Rowe Well in 1901, about the time the Grand Canyon Railway reached the South Rim. Rowe Well would expand in later years to include a tourist camp, bowling alley, and dance hall.

the political and business power of railroads in this period. In the interim, the Camerons built the Grand View Hotel, completing it in 1897. The Santa Fe bought them out in 1926 after the conclusion of the legal battles.

J. W. Thurber, possibly in partnership with Captain Hance, began to build the Bright Angel Hotel in 1896 and finally finished it in 1900. It started out as a building from another location; he moved it to the site and later added a second floor. The hotel became the centerpiece of the hodgepodge Bright Angel Camp. Sold about 1902 to the Santa Fe, Martin Buggeln managed it until 1905. It remained in place until 1935, when the railroad demolished it to make way for the Bright Angel Lodge.

Several other people came to the canyon during this time to establish tourist-related businesses. Beginning in 1889, John Verkamp sold general merchandise and tourist items from a tent. As with the tourist accommodations that came before him, this established method, with its low overhead, served him well, and his business prospered for seven years. In 1905, he began construction of Verkamp's Curios. The March 18, 1905, issue of the *Williams News* noted:

> The United States has granted to John G. Verkamp, of Flagstaff, the right to one acre of land near the big hotel [El Tovar] at Grand Canyon, with the right to construct a building for a "curio" business. It is rumored that Mr. Verkamp will begin at once to construct an elegant building on said land.

John Verkamp opened his doors on January 31, 1906, and his store and business remained in the family until 2009. The family lived in the upstairs quarters of the store. Imagine growing up with the Grand Canyon as your front yard. Little changed over the years, but the building did go through a major facelift in 1989. It still anchors the east end of the Historic District, as the National Park Service purchased the building and opened it in 2009 as a visitor center and Grand Canyon Association bookstore.

A pair of Grand Canyon legends arrived after the railroad did, and they established another notable business. Emery and Ellsworth Kolb moved their photography shop from Williams to the canyon in 1903. The Kolb brothers' presence had a considerable effect, as they had a running squabble with the Santa Fe and Fred Harvey Companies, which wanted their business, and with the park service, which just wanted them out. The Santa Fe built Lookout Studio behind the Bright

Kolb Studio, circa 1904, at the head of the Bright Angel Trail. Note the tollgate.

Angel Lodge at the request of the Harvey Company in an attempt to keep business away from Kolb Studio. However, this turned out to be one occasion where the powerful railroad and Harvey Company were not to have their way.

The Kolbs, in an agreement with Ralph Cameron, originally ran their studio from a tent on the edge of the rim just to the west of the Bright Angel Hotel. It over-looked the head of the Bright Angel Trail, so it made sense to relocate, in 1904, to the tollhouse the Cam-erons had built. This location gave them a monopoly on taking photographs of tourists going down the trail on Cameron's, and later Fred Harvey's, mules. Harvey management saw a loss of revenue and did everything in their power to dislodge the Kolbs, from political maneu-vering to outright slander.

The Harvey Company had taken on a worthy oppo-nent. The Kolbs were there to stay. They built their origi-nal studio in 1904 and added to it in 1915 and 1925. When Emery Kolb died in 1976, at the age of nine-ty-five, the building was still there and he had been living in it and running the studio all that time. Kolb Studio is now owned by the National Park Service. The Grand Canyon Association funded its restoration and manages it as a gallery and bookstore. Emery would probably approve of this artistic venue that hosts a variety of art and photography shows. Kolbs' historic structure will be a part of the canyon scene for many years to come.

The Babbitt Brothers Trading Company arrived in 1905. This operation also opened in a tent, where it sold general merchandise. In 1921, the Santa Fe built a store for the company that stood across the tracks from the present depot. It has since been replaced by a mod-ern supermarket operated by a concessioner.

From the time of its arrival in September 1901, main-tenance and rebuilding of the Grand Canyon Railway never seemed to stop. Although the railway operated legally as a separate company with the power to make its own contracts, hire and fire, and publish its own timetables, it remained a part of the Atchison, Topeka

and Santa Fe Railway Company. Engineering draw-ings of structures at the canyon might have one or the other company listed in the legend, but the money and resources all came from the same place.

The parent Atchison, Topeka and Santa Fe Compa-ny brought to bear much of its facilities, engineering staff, and equipment to the Grand Canyon Railway. With some notable exceptions, the Santa Fe bridge and building crews built and maintained the vast majority of the structures at the canyon. They first built the board and batten station to the north of the main line tracks, across from the legs of the wye. The railroad had a twenty-acre station grant, and it needed every bit of it for the planned station and yards. Eventually the com-pany constructed and maintained over 600 structures at the South Rim.

In 1904, the Santa Fe introduced the Fred Harvey Company to the Grand Canyon. Since the 1870s, Har-vey had been running the depot hotels and restaurants for the Santa Fe on a verbal agreement sealed with a handshake. Lawyers for both companies formalized this arrangement in 1891 after a short court battle, result-ing in a written agreement that also called for the Fred Harvey Company to provide dining car service on all of the Santa Fe trains.

The Harvey Company came to the canyon at full throttle. They, along with the board of directors of the Atchison, Topeka and Santa Fe, determined to make the first major project, El Tovar Hotel, a showplace. Santa Fe management wanted to clean up and organize Grand Canyon Village in accordance with their plan to elimi-nate the competition. As they discovered, this wasn't the way things would turn out.

El Tovar Hotel, pictured here in 1907, offered such luxuries as a solarium, rooftop garden, music, wine, and billiard rooms, and an art gallery.
||||||||||||||||||||

El Tovar should have been named after a lieutenant of Francisco Coronado's expedition to Grand Canyon. Don Garcia Lopez de Cardenas became the first non-Indian to see the Grand Canyon, in 1540, but a hotel in Trinidad, Colorado, was already named after him. So the Santa Fe named the South Rim hotel after his superior, who had never seen the canyon. Don Pedro de Tovar would have been proud of the magnificent structure bearing his name.

Up to this time, the Santa Fe built its depots and Harvey Houses of functional stone, brick, or board and batten construction. El Tovar became the first major departure from these styles. Proudly described in a Santa Fe brochure after opening in 1905, El Tovar was then, and is now, a beautiful building resting near the rim of the canyon.

El Tovar is a long, low, rambling edifice, built of native boulders and pine logs from far-off Oregon. The width north and south is three hundred and twenty-seven feet and from east to west two hundred and eighteen feet....The hotel is from three to four stories high. It contains more than a hundred bedrooms.... Ample accommodations are provided for 250 guests....Outside are wide porches and roof gardens.... El Tovar is more than a hotel; it is a village devoted to the entertainment of travelers.

Not bad for the wilds of the Arizona Territory. El Tovar has endured as the flagship hotel at Grand Canyon and celebrated its 100th birthday in 2005.

Building this hotel at the Grand Canyon must have put considerable strain on the contractor. For the most part, supplies came from Williams. The Polson Brothers store had a standing order for materials to be delivered weekly to the canyon by rail. One item never changed during the course of construction. A case of "good scotch" apparently helped to fortify the contractor for his daily trials and tribulations. As the Polsons did not stock liquor, a clerk purchased the whiskey weekly from one of the local saloons and put it on the train with the rest of the order. One might wonder how the contractor billed the Santa Fe for these "essential materials."

Canyon facilities needed electric power and steam for light and heat. To provide these services, the railroad constructed a boiler house and pumping plant next to the tracks and south of El Tovar. Originally built in 1905, these facilities were enlarged in 1911 and again in 1913 as the village grew. The plant lasted until 1926, when the Santa Fe erected a new power plant. By 1924, the National Park Service had devised a master plan for Grand Canyon Village. It required a new powerhouse to meet the demands of the rapidly expanding park, and the park service recommended to the Atchison, Topeka and Santa Fe that one be built as soon as possible. Wasting no time, the railroad engineers began the planning and building almost immediately after receiving the temporary permits to do so.

The Santa Fe laid water and steam lines to the buildings throughout the village even before the construction of the powerhouse began. Concrete and steel construction with a natural limestone exterior formed the major structure. Limestone from the tail of the wye and from other locations within the park allowed this relatively large building to blend in as much as possible with the local setting.

Only one part of this complex did not fit in—the more than 200-foot smokestack. This sore thumb defiled the natural scene until the plant closed in 1956 and the smokestack was torn down—for the second, and last, time.

During construction of the stack in 1926, Santa Fe

Harvey Girls like these three on a locomotive in front of the Williams Harvey House frequently visited the canyon.

engineers realized it was a hazard, so far out of plumb you could see the tilt. They tore it down and started over. Although the smokestack looked ugly, smoke from the steam boilers and the huge diesel motors for the generators needed to be dispersed away from the community. Power today comes from hydroelectric sources north of the canyon, on the Colorado River near Page, Arizona. The powerhouse is now used as a storage facility, but thankfully the smokestack no longer violates aesthetics.

Oddly enough, the power plant never produced pollution at levels that visually obscured the canyon. Built without scrubbers, the coal-fired plant in Page became a constant source of smoke and haze, however. It has since installed scrubbers, and visibility has significantly improved.

The power plant, when in operation, provided some lighter moments. Every day at 8:00 a.m., noon, 1:00 p.m., and 5:00 p.m., the whistle blew to signal the start of the workday, lunch, and quitting time. Tourists, startled by the whistle, asked, "What's that?" "Oh that's just the steamboat pulling into the dock on the river," the locals replied. With that, the tourists headed for the rim to see the steamboat.

During the early years at Grand Canyon, a doctor attended to the medical needs of residents and tourists in a carbody office located at the end-of-track on the south side of the yards. At this minimal facility, the doctor gave physical examinations, treated minor illnesses, and provided emergency treatment prior to sending the patient on to Williams or Flagstaff. When the Santa Fe built a hospital in 1929, the level of medical care improved considerably, but doctors continued to use the

Mary Colter and Santa Fe Railroad officials standing in the tramway gondola near Lookout Studio, circa 1931.

carbody for office visits well into the 1930s.

In 1902, the Harvey Company made a decision that had far-reaching effects on Grand Canyon Village and other tourist facilities at the canyon. They hired Mary Elizabeth Jane Colter as an architect and interior designer. She stamped her indelible imprint on the Santa Fe and Harvey Companies with her version of a natural style of Pueblo Indian architecture.

El Tovar received her distinctive touch when she came on the scene in 1905. Designing the cocktail lounge in her trademark style, she then experimented and practiced before she began work on her first major structure at the canyon, Hopi House. Colter used inspiration from the Hopi culture and designed the building to look like a pueblo. At the direction of the Harvey Company, the Santa Fe built Hopi House between El Tovar and

Hopi House not only sold Native American rugs and jewelry, Hopi artisans also lived in the upper floor of the building.

Verkamp's Curios to provide direct competition with Verkamp's. Completed in 1905, it served for many years as the focal point of Indian dances put on by Porter Tomichi and his Hopi family. These dances provided an important part of Santa Fe and Fred Harvey advertising. To this end, the railroad constructed an Indian dance platform next to Hopi House in October 1951.

Colter's next efforts came in 1914, when she designed and built Lookout Studio and Hermits Rest. As previously noted, the Santa Fe constructed Lookout Studio at the request of the Harvey Company to provide direct competition to Kolb Studio. Colter surely did not have this in mind when she designed a roughly contoured building that almost blended in with the edge of the rim. It is an example of the art that a fine architect can produce. She created Hermits Rest in the same unobtrusive manner. Built at the end of West Rim Drive, it fits in with the rim almost as if it came to be there naturally. These may well be two of Colter's finest works.

Phantom Ranch, in the bottom of the canyon where

Bright Angel Creek meets the Colorado River, received her attentions in 1922. She designed Phantom Ranch to accommodate the mule passengers and hikers on the Bright Angel and Kaibab Trails. In 1934, a swimming pool built next to the creek and fed by its waters offered a refreshing place to swim. Over the years, Phantom Ranch has been updated; it is still in use today and well worth the trip. Although the inner canyon is a place of beauty, it can be a harsh and changing environment. Probably due to its rustic and sturdy construction, Phantom Ranch withstood the power of a major flood on Bright Angel Creek in 1966. Sadly, the swimming pool did not survive the flood, and it has not been rebuilt.

Desert View Watchtower, probably Colter's most famous work at the canyon, stands near the easternmost limit of the park. Perched on the rim and overlooking the eastern stretches of the canyon and the junction of the Little Colorado River with the Colorado, the tower

Lookout Studio's flat roof, stacked stone walls, and peeled-log timbers mimic the architecture of twelfth-century Puebloan people.

Although Desert View Watchtower appears to be made entirely of Kaibab Limestone, the Santa Fe bridge department constructed a steel skeleton as a foundation for the structure.

provides a fantastic view in every direction. Arizona's highest mountains, the San Francisco Peaks, can be seen to the south. At 12,633 feet high and seventy miles south, they appear to be but a short distance on a clear day. No farther away are the multicolored formations of the Painted Desert. Stretching across the horizon, these ribbons of color make the short climb to the top of the tower worth every step. Here, too, for many years the Hopi put on snake dances to entertain the tourists.

In 1935, Bright Angel Hotel was showing its age when Colter turned her talents to its renovation. She totally changed the concept, demolishing the old hotel. Slowly, the new lodge began to take shape. Several of the original structures on the site had a rustic charm that Colter wanted to maintain, underscoring her appreciation for things historic. She made use of existing log buildings such as Buckey O'Neill's cabin and the original Grand Canyon post office by incorporating them into the overall plan. Logs and wood became her primary medium here instead of natural rock. The hand-squared logs of the old cabins probably provided her inspiration. In the lodge itself, a geological fireplace with representative natural stone from every layer in the canyon formed her signature masterpiece. The separate cabins, including the old post office, offer private accommodations and are reminiscent of the old tent camp. When Colter had finished, Bright Angel Lodge looked new but it already possessed a history.

Her next and last projects at the canyon came in 1936 and 1937. The men's and women's dormitories helped to alleviate the chronic housing shortage for Harvey employees at the South Rim. Employees who work in the hotel service trades reside at these dorms.

The Harvey Company held considerable respect for Colter's work at the canyon. Therefore, they considered it quite fitting to name the women's dormitory in her honor, and Colter Hall still bears her name today. Although Mary Colter's work came to a close at the canyon with these projects, her work with the Atchison, Topeka and Santa Fe and Fred Harvey Companies continued.

Ralph Cameron still charged one dollar per animal on the Bright Angel Trail, but the Harvey Company ran tours along the rim in horse-drawn carriages and sent guided mule trips down the Hermit Trail. The Santa Fe completed horse and mule barns in 1907, along with a blacksmith shop to service these animals. In these early years, Martin Buggeln ran the livery business for the Atchison, Topeka and Santa Fe and Fred Harvey. His prior expertise in this field made him a natural for the position.

Hotels, camps, and dining facilities have always been important considerations at the South Rim. Although the scenery is the reason for coming to the canyon, everyone needs a place to stay and eat. However, one area of concern always will take precedence over any and all others at the South Rim.

Water remains one of the most vital issues for Grand Canyon National Park. Initially, the railroad hauled water from Williams in tank cars. Every train literally carried enough water for the passengers on board. After the railroad built cisterns, water specials made the trip to the canyon on demand, with fewer cars in the winter and more in the summer. Old photographs of the railyard almost always include water cars in the background on a siding. A water delivery track, number 4,

at the west end of the yards, serviced the hotels. Later, the Santa Fe moved water operations to the south side of the yard, opposite the new station. Track 21 had a flume alongside, which from 1911 to 1925 fed water via gravity from the cars to storage tanks. Later, the railroad built a water delivery track to the east of the stem of the wye and designated it track 35. Pipes with hose connections for fourteen cars transferred the water to steel storage tanks.

All of this water came from Flagstaff, Bellemont, or the primary source, Del Rio. Del Rio (later changed to Puro) is a station on the "Peavine," the Ash Fork to Phoenix run. Spanish for "from the river," Del Rio is located in one of the few valleys in northern Arizona with a year-round supply of water. This source is 122 rail miles from the canyon, and the Santa Fe used it until the sixties. The Atchison, Topeka and Santa Fe hauled wa-

A supplemental water train from Puro, Arizona, dumps 204,000 gallons into the park system on August 7, 1961.

ter to the park for railroad customers and residents at cost, just as it did for the ranchers. Few, if any, railroads have been so willing to provide a service to customers on this scale (up to 250,000 gallons per trainload). The Santa Fe could have charged enough to make a profit and did not.

Water conservation has always been a primary concern of the inhabitants of the canyon and for the railroad. To this end, the engineering staff of the Atchison, Topeka and Santa Fe designed and built a water reclamation plant in 1926. Hailed as a major engineering achievement, it drew visitors from around the world who were interested in water reclamation projects. The railroad expanded the plant's capacity in 1934 to meet the needs of the soon-to-be-completed Bright Angel Lodge. It's still in operation today.

Never designed to provide drinking water, it merely turned wastewater into usable water for the locomotives, vegetation, and the sanitary facilities in the village. Good sense dictated that drinking water should not be used for these purposes. Not too many places in this world have pink and blue water pipes, but Grand Canyon Village does. Water for drinking and general human consumption is delivered by the blue pipes. Delivery to the locomotives, vegetation, and the sanitary conveniences is made via the pink pipes. In this way, it is a simple matter for the maintenance people to identify the proper line and not mix the two water sources.

As admirable as this engineering achievement is, it did not solve the water problems at the canyon. Indian Garden, below the South Rim on the Bright Angel Trail, usually has a reliable supply of water. The problem of how to get the water 2,000 feet up to the rim required

some new technology and again, the Santa Fe engineering department went to work. In 1931, they built a pump house and a pipeline from Indian Garden to the South Rim. Before they could begin the construction, they had to build a cable tramway to haul equipment and materials to the site. The water line required a total of two and a half miles of pipe installed from the pump house up the wall of the South Rim. After completion of the project, they removed the tram.

When the Santa Fe completed this engineering marvel and put it into operation in 1932, Grand Canyon Village had a good supply of water. The Indian Garden pipeline eliminated the need for a regular water train. However, when required maintenance of the system shut the pipeline down or when people used more water than the system could provide, the dispatcher scheduled water extras from Puro. Railroad water supply on an "as needed" basis continued until 1968, when the park service got its transcanyon pipeline from Roaring Springs into regular operation. Even with these supply systems, water conservation and reuse at the canyon remains a high priority.

With operations at the South Rim well under way in 1907, the Atchison, Topeka and Santa Fe began another project at the south end of the line, in Williams. Construction started on a much needed Harvey House, restaurant, and depot. The original Harvey facility, comprised of several boxcars with lunch counters across from the station, left a lot to be desired. The Fray Marcos Hotel replaced this with a first-class establishment. On the interior, the hotel contained the usual Harvey southwestern trappings, but the exterior did not reflect the usual style of the company. It defies precise classification. Depending on which architect describes the structure, it has been called Greek revival, classic revival, or Beaux-Arts. Whatever the correct designation, the Fray Marcos is not the traditional Harvey style.

Designed in 1905 and constructed in 1907, the Fray Marcos opened for service on March 10, 1908. Architect Francis W. Wilson of Santa Barbara designed the building for the Santa Fe Railway. It is the earliest known and oldest existing reinforced poured concrete building in Arizona. The Fred Harvey Company managed the hotel and restaurant.

An interesting note about the original design is reflected in its flat, poured concrete roof. Wilson was not knowledgeable about northern Arizona winters and the snow loads that storms can generate. It did not take

long for the roof to leak like a sieve when accumulated snow melted and worked its way through the obliging concrete. Instead of spending the money for wooden or metal framing to peak the roof and drain off the water, the Santa Fe hoisted tons of readily available volcanic cinders onto the roof, formed them into peaks, and added a covering of asphalt roofing. Oddly enough, for as long as the railroad maintained the asphalt roofing, it remained intact. As the building became derelict in later years, water poured through the structure and caused considerable damage that proved very costly to fix.

When the doors opened for business, the hotel and restaurant provided train passengers, tourists, and Williams residents with the high-quality service and meals for which the Harvey Company was known. It also

ıııııııııııııııııııııııı
The Fray Marcos Hotel and Williams train station about 1910. People generally referred to this as the Williams Harvey House.

Seated dining area of the Williams Harvey House, which was separated by a wall from the lunch counter.

became the centerpiece of Williams's social life. Harvey Girls served meals at the lunch counter or in the dining room. A curio shop offered Indian goods and other items.

The original design had accommodations for guests in twenty-two rooms and another ten rooms for staff, all on the second floor. Room 5 is a two-room suite with its own bath and overlooks the tracks. Rooms 7 and 8 and 13 and 14 have a shared bath. Guests in all other rooms used a community bath and toilet. The Santa Fe made several changes and additions to the original building over the years. The first, as early as 1909, upgraded utilities and facilities and cost $35,000. Company carpenters and masons handled all additions and renovations. A two-story addition in 1925 gave the hotel an additional twenty-one rooms. Built in adjoining pairs, twenty of the rooms have a private bath.

They included a two-room suite with a fireplace on the northwest corner of the addition as an apartment for the hotel manager.

The Fray Marcos for many years anchored the southern end of the Grand Canyon line. Retired by the Santa Fe in 1954, the hotel remained dormant while the station continued to service the east-west main line and Williams–Grand Canyon train traffic. Although technically retired, parts of the hotel did see use by crews building the Johnson Canyon bypass in 1960–61. The Williams Elks Club leased it from March 1, 1963, to April 1, 1983. Their contract gave them use of the kitchen, dining area, lobby, and curio room. Santa Fe maintenance crews and the field engineer used the station facility until 1988.

Rehabilitation by the Grand Canyon Railway Company began on March 29, 1989. Initial plans called for portions of the Fray Marcos Hotel to be used as a passenger facility for its steam trains headed to the Grand Canyon. It also functioned as a museum dedicated to the historical preservation of the railroad and the cultural history of the region. Future plans called for the second floor to be renovated as company offices. Time, with its inevitable changes, has taken so many of the wonderful old Harvey Houses from us. At least we did not lose this one.

With most of the building at the canyon and Williams completed, the Atchison, Topeka and Santa Fe and Harvey Companies settled down to mostly routine maintenance. Railroad paint and repair crews took care of most of this work. Section gangs handled the yard work for required track realignments, rail and tie changes, and ballasting. Not much changed at the South Rim of the Grand Canyon. The park service added new public facilities and roads from time to time, but the Atchison, Topeka and Santa Fe and Harvey Companies continued business as usual until 1954. At this time, Santa Fe management decided to get out of the hotel business at the Grand Canyon. This decision resulted in the sale of all existing commercial facilities to the Fred Harvey Company, and the donation of the powerhouse, utility systems, and water systems to the National Park Service. The only major changes after the sale occurred when the Harvey Company built a couple of motor hotels that still draw criticism.

With this sale, an era came to an end. The Santa Fe still owned the right-of-way and the station facilities at the Grand Canyon, but it no longer held an interest in the hotel business. Passenger revenues steadily declined, but the Grand Canyon Railway continued to advertise the park as a primary attraction.

Cash transport is one service that did not change as long as the trains continued to run. Until fairly recently, Grand Canyon Village did not have a bank. As considerable cash was taken in during the course of the day at all of the Harvey-run facilities, the Santa Fe devised a means of handling it safely and securely. At the end of the day, the accounting office, located downstairs in El Tovar, totaled up the cash, carried it to the Santa Fe cashier at the station, and traded it in for an American Express traveler's check. This check usually amounted to something in the neighborhood of $25,000 to $30,000 during the summer months in the 1950s. The agent placed the cash, which included bags of silver dollars brought by tourists from Las Vegas, in the safe at the station until the train left that evening. Just prior to the train's departure, the baggageman signed for the cash and locked it in a special container on the baggage car. Never in all the years the Santa Fe transferred cash from the Grand Canyon to Los Angeles did a loss occur. There were no "great train robberies" or even an attempt to hijack one of these shipments. But, just in case, the baggageman had an old .38 revolver available. However, no one ever maintained it or checked to see if it was loaded or even worked. Fortunately, it was never needed or used.

What can best describe the relationship of the Santa Fe to the Grand Canyon? Maybe this: *Veni, vidi, vici.* I came, I saw, I conquered. Add to that *Ego edificavi*: I built. Now it is up to us to preserve this architectural legacy. The Grand Canyon Village Historic District helps to ensure these monuments to another time will not be destroyed. Their preservation guarantees us, and our descendants, a window to the past. It is a remarkable window. Come and enjoy the view.

Saginaw Southern Shay locomotives with log cars, 1897.

LOGGING AT APEX

LUMBER WAS ONE OF ARIZONA'S PRIMARY industries for many decades. Most people outside of Arizona think of the state as one vast desert wasteland. This is hardly the case. The world's largest stand of ponderosa pine prospers here. A diagonal band of these great trees stretches across Arizona from the South Rim of the Grand Canyon southwest along the Mogollon Rim to the New Mexico border. Williams sits smack in the middle of this beautiful forest. The Grand Canyon Railway runs in and out of stands of ponderosas at either end of its run from Williams to the canyon.

Railroads have always needed timber. As surely as trains run on steel, they also run on timber. A thirty-nine-foot rail requires twenty-five ties to support it. Depending on the method of preservation, its location, and the loads carried on the line, a tie can be expected to last from five to twenty years in normal service.

Part of an article in the May 16, 1903, issue of the *Williams News* stated: "It has been ascertained that each mile of the 250,000 miles of railway in the United States requires 400 ties per year. It takes fifty years to grow a tree that will make three ties, and ordinarily requires twenty-five acres to furnish 400 ties." The larger ponderosas in Arizona could easily do better than this.

With this in mind, the Saginaw Lumber Company of Saginaw, Michigan, came to Williams and on February 14, 1893, secured timber rights in what is now the Kaibab National Forest. They wasted no time: they had a lumber mill under construction in April 1893 and in operation by June of that year. These hardy logging Swedes of Michigan brought their particular brand of hard work with them.

Business boomed, with lumber in demand by local Williams businesses, ranchers, and the railroad. The lumber company arrived a year after the Atlantic and Pacific Railroad began its transit across the high desert of northern Arizona. Continued construction on the new roadbed demanded thousands of ties that Saginaw readily provided.

These industrious people, not content with only

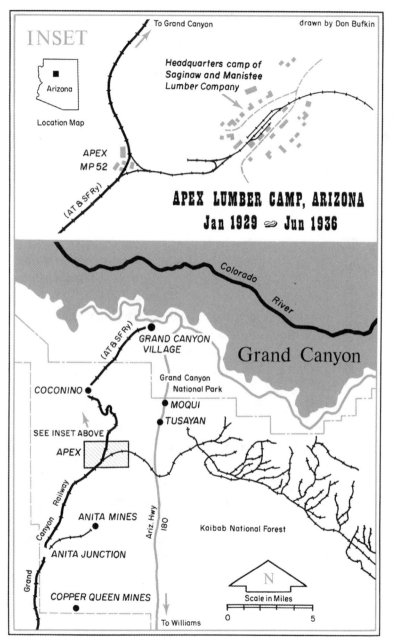

supplying ties and lumber, built and opened a box factory adjacent to the mill in January 1894. The expanding farm industry in the valleys to the south, around Phoenix, provided their main business, with an increasing need for produce shooks. Fire leveled the factory in June 1897, but the company rebuilt in short order.

The Saginaw's primary timber leases lay in the areas south of Williams. Loggers worked these stands with the fervor of beavers. Evidence of their work is still with us in the form of abandoned logging railroad grades, which became the U.S. Forest Service roads that give us access to these magnificent woodlands.

Business was good enough that Saginaw decided to expand its operations. This required additional capital, and the Manistee Lumber Company of Manistee, Michigan, became a willing partner. The merger of these two logging and lumber concerns created the Saginaw and Manistee Lumber Company of Arizona in 1899.

The mill's location in Williams made it very convenient for this company to supply the ties and lumber needs of the Santa Fe and Grand Canyon Railroad during construction. In later years, reconstruction of the Grand Canyon line and the heavy requirements for ties by the Santa Fe again caused the company to expand the mill facilities. This mill provided up to five million ties per year to fill the railroad's requirements. Mining timber, for the mines at Anita and other

Saginaw and Manistee Lumber Company mill and box plant in Williams.
BELOW: Loggers at Apex circa 1930. Most of the men pictured here are either Swedish or Swedish-American.

claims in the Francis District, also came from this mill. During the building boom at Grand Canyon Village, the Saginaw and Manistee supplied most of the construction lumber for the hotels and other buildings. The lumber company therefore became tied to the railroad from its beginnings. Ironically, although the mill provided material for construction and maintenance of the railroad at the outset, Saginaw and Manistee did not use the Grand Canyon line for shipment of logs for nearly another three decades.

Forest Service timber leases determined the company's logging operations. Areas south of Williams and in the Chalender and Garland Prairie Districts in the Kaibab National Forest continued to be logged. The company also held the leases for the Bellemont District of the Coconino National Forest, which they logged

in the 1920s. All of these areas are between Williams and Flagstaff.

Those Swedes were an efficient bunch. So efficient, in fact, that they finished these leases in less than thirty years. Not that they destroyed the forest, but the loggers had cut their allotted timber very systematically, and the mill and box plant had also kept up with the demands of their customers. The Saginaw and Manistee needed a new timber lease.

New breath came from the Kaibab National Forest in what is now called the Tusayan District. During the early 1900s, the U.S. Forest Service referred to this area as the Anita-Moqui District, and later on the Grand Canyon District. On August 2, 1928, after the granting of timber rights, the Saginaw and Manistee Lumber Company contracted with the Atchison, Topeka and Santa Fe Railway Company for grading of tracks and sidings at Apex and for rental of fifty-six-pound relay rail.

Williams in the 1940s. The railroad yards are in the foreground with the roundhouse (**LOWER RIGHT**), and the Saginaw and Manistee mill and box plant (**RIGHT CENTER**).

Construction began on a wye with a twenty-seven-car north leg, a fifty-eight-car south leg, and a twenty-seven-car siding on the south leg. They built the turnouts in conjunction with the existing thirty-one-car siding on the east side of the main line. Eventually, this wye fed into twenty-six miles of main line and spur track to the east of Apex and just to the south of Grand Canyon National Park. More important, it led to a community of people who lived, worked, and moved with the job of cutting logs. About one mile east of Apex, the company located the headquarters camp for the Saginaw and Manistee operations on the east and west slopes of a small valley.

Virtually everything in this community arrived by rail from Bellemont and Garland Prairie. Housing for the single men looked like small wooden boxcars without wheels. Workers loaded two of these on flatcars or one to a log car for transportation to end of track, where they established the logging camps. The company provided the management and the families with larger housing. Arvid Anderson, the camp superintendent, had the largest house, consisting of a living room, kitchen, and two bedrooms. Family housing included a living room, kitchen, and one bedroom. All of these homes sat on temporary wooden and stone foundations still visible today. One unique feature of these houses is that they came apart at the middle for transport, and workers rejoined them in their original *L* or *T* configuration at the destination. These truly mobile homes provided reasonably comfortable living for their occupants.

Five houses on the west slope and five more on the east slope made up the initial living quarters of the headquarters camp. Several sheds and buildings for

Lumberjacks using a two-man saw to fell a ponderosa pine tree in 1929.

The Matson family in front of their moveable home at Apex. Mr. Matson operated the steam loader.

track had its turnout at the north end. A shorter spur on the east side, with room for two locomotives and tenders, had its turnout on the south end. This spur contained a pit for doing maintenance on the underside of the locomotives. The wye at the south end of the camp enabled locomotives to turn around without making the trip up to the Santa Fe siding at Apex.

Logging families included children, and they needed an education. It mattered little to these people that they lived in the middle of a forest. Apex was home, and that's where the school needed to be. In the fall of 1929, Apex School District Number 3 opened classes in a one-room schoolhouse fashioned from two boxcars set on a substantial timber foundation. Margaret Longley from Flagstaff accepted the teacher's position and was prepared to teach grades one through eight. All of this became her domain for the munificent sum of $130 per month, plus board. In 1931, Katherine Shipp, also of Flagstaff, succeeded Margaret for that school year. The following year, Rose Wilson came from back east to teach in the northern wilds of Arizona. The climate must have been agreeable, as she stayed until the school closed, in the spring of 1936.

Rose Wilson had quite a forceful personality. An excellent teacher, the students remembered her most for her stern and forthright manner. To her, everything had a right way and a wrong way. Ask any of her students, and they would tell you her name is Rose B. Wilson. Not Miss Wilson, not Rose Wilson, but most emphatically Rose B. Wilson. They might have been in the middle of a forest, but as far as she was concerned, her students would be taught properly.

Classes never exceeded fifteen pupils, and the students

working on the locomotives and for other company business occupied positions in the valley by the tracks. Spurs along the valley allowed for the spotting of the commissary car, kitchen, and dining cars, and the supervisor's car from time to time, as needed. Usually supervisors traveled with the loggers to the end of track. Two oil tanks and a water tank on the west slope serviced the locomotives.

A gravity-feed line from a siding between Apex on the railroad and the headquarters camp supplied drinking water. The Santa Fe spotted water tank cars there and hooked them up to the water line.

Primarily used for the work train, the longest of two spurs located in the valley occupied the west side of the main logging line. Built for a capacity of seven cars, this

Dirt track spur leading to the cutting area in the Anita-Moqui District.
Note the lack of ballast and stacked logs to the left.

Teacher Rose B. Wilson with her class at Apex school in 1934.

rarely filled all eight grades. The school stood above the camp on the west slope of the valley, and because of its relatively small size, it provided a warm and friendly atmosphere. Students made lasting friendships. For the time, this school and its companion school at Anita (District Number 7) were unique in one regard: they were unsegregated. Williams, forty-five miles south of Anita and fifty-two miles south of Apex, had segregated schools for the Anglos and Mexicans, but the Apex and Anita schools accepted Mexican and Indian students from the section gangs on the Santa Fe. As the years progressed further into the Depression, diversity of the school population would go through quite a few changes.

The Saginaw and Manistee had its origins in Swedish-American culture. Mexicans and others worked in the mill and box plant, but in the camps, the predominant worker had either been born in Sweden or in the United States of Swedish parents. As time went on, Norwegians and Finns began to arrive in the camps. During the thirties, hard times prevailed in the Midwest. In addition, Okies, Arkies, and Louisianans began their trek to the West in search of work and a better life. All of these good people had been accustomed to hard work, but circumstances beyond their control dictated that they move on. No strangers to long, hard days, they fit in to the logging camps very well. Apex became a melting pot. Here a man earned his keep and maintained his self-respect while doing an honest day's work for a decent wage. The workers' families met and got to know different kinds of people, people they had never had the chance to know before.

Weather permitting, logging continued year-round. Heavy snowfalls in some years suspended operations until enough snow melted away to allow the lumberjacks to resume cutting. The main line of the Saginaw and Manistee logging railroad at Apex can only be called a dirt track road, with temporary spurs to the cutting areas. Company section gangs normally laid ties directly on the cleared ground without ballast. Stumps of freshly cut trees came up between the ties in many places. The ties were Santa Fe rejects from the mill in Williams because the company considered the line to be temporary. Ties sank into wet ground and did not provide firm footing for the trains; even when the ground dried out, they shifted laterally and the roadbed remained unstable. Enginemen considered this road a real challenge to run.

The "dinky skinners," as the "real" railroad hogheads called the logging engineers, had a tougher time of daily operations than did their main line brethren.

Usually the locomotive swayed from side to side so badly that the crew found it very difficult to maintain balance. Derailments occurred almost daily, but usually the locomotive didn't roll over because the engineers operated under reduced speeds as a matter of necessity. These dinky skinners used rerailing frogs as a standard tool of the trade. Most of the time, all they needed to get the locomotive back on the track were some rail, frogs, and hard work.

All of the hogheads had come from the old country, and they still had their Swedish accents. One told the story of a derailment he had experienced. As the engineer was running down the main line light (engine and tender only), the locomotive began to rock considerably from side to side. When he approached a curve, he real-

Cat skinner skidding logs to the loading area with the aid of an arch. **BELOW**: Saginaw and Manistee Lumber Company logging camp No. 36 in the Grand Canyon District.

ized the locomotive would derail, so he braked and told the fireman to jump, as he thought they might roll over. The other man made it off, and when the hoghead tried to "join the birds," the violent swaying of the engine threw him back into the cab. In the excitement of telling this story, his accent came out. "The damn ting was rockin' so bad I yumped twice before I got off the damn ting." Fortunately, the locomotive stayed upright and he and the fireman only had some scratches and bruises to show for their flight. Several hours of hard work got the engine back on the tracks.

The Saginaw and Manistee dinky skinners had three locomotives with which to work. Two Baldwin 2-6-0s and a two-truck Shay made up the power roster for the company at Apex. All oil fired, the Baldwins carried numbers 2 and 3 and the Shay was number 4. Everyone in the camps referred to them as either the 2, 3, or 4 Spot.

Built in 1904 for the Saginaw and Manistee, number 2 came out of the factory with the name "Aug. Lindstrom," for the company president. Originally numbered 23883 at the factory, it saw extensive use in company operations at Bellemont, Chalender, Garland

Baldwin factory photograph of 2-6-0 locomotive Aug. Lindstrom. This became the Saginaw and Manistee 2 Spot.

Saginaw and Manistee logging train with 2-6-0 Baldwin 3 Spot and steam loader.

Prairie, and areas south of Williams as well as Apex. The company eventually sold it for scrap during World War II.

Also built for the Saginaw and Manistee, number 3 rolled off the production line in 1907. Numbered 32249 at the factory, it is unknown if it had been named. The 3 Spot became the backup engine for the Grand Canyon District operations. It also saw service in the other districts logged by the company. When the company completed cutting on the Grand Canyon District in 1936, this locomotive remained on the spur of the headquarters camp at Apex until scrapped in 1941 by Mallin Brothers of Prescott.

Number 4 came to the Saginaw and Manistee in 1923 by way of the Arizona Lumber and Timber Company. Built in 1913 for the Flagstaff Lumber and Manufacturing Company and numbered 2732 by Lima as a 50-2 class Shay, this locomotive became extensively damaged in a derailment, and Flagstaff Lumber Manufacturing probably sold it to Arizona Lumber and Timber in 1917. The 4 Spot carried Arizona Lumber and Timber number 7 prior to coming to Saginaw and Manistee. As with the others, it saw service in all of the districts in operation by the company prior to making the trip to the Grand Canyon District. Equipped with gear-driven wheels, it had more power than the rod engines, and its working environment became the steeper grades and heavier loads the Baldwins couldn't handle. When cutting came to a close at Apex, number 4 was worn out. The crew spotted her on the water siding at Apex to await the cutting torch in 1941.

Technically, it can be said that the original three locomotives saw service on the Grand Canyon line, but only two made the transit from Williams to Apex, and the other made one round-trip. When they came up the line with the bag and baggage of the Saginaw and Manistee, it must have been a sight to behold. Flats with houses followed, along with tanks, log cars with shacks, steam loaders, logging wheels, tractors, and the headquarters camp cars. One could almost liken it to a circus train, but the Saginaw and Manistee came to Apex for serious business. These people did not represent a traveling circus in any way.

After making the initial move and getting operations under way, the daily routine of work became the way of life in the logging camps. Initial cutting was headquartered out of Apex, and as the cutting progressed east, so did the logging camps. They sprang up along the

Saginaw and Manistee Shay 4 Spot during loading operations on Skinner Ridge.

main line, and each in turn had to be dismantled when the camp moved. By the time the company suspended cutting operations in 1936, a total of thirty-eight camps had appeared and disappeared.

Apex remained the headquarters and maintenance camp for the duration. All major work on the locomotives, tractors, and trucks had to be handled there, in the company shops. Hostlers lubricated the locomotives and kept steam up all night long so that they were ready to roll in the morning. If a locomotive spent the night in an advance camp, a hostler went with it. Work on the skid cats (caterpillar tractors) and trucks had to be completed at night in order for the logging crews to keep up with the cutting schedules. In the winter, mechanics drained the radiators every night, as they had no antifreeze. The maintenance men filled them again in the morning and warmed up the engines in time to have them ready to go at first light.

The logging crews' day started at 5:00 a.m. with breakfast. Felling trees and bucking logs with hand tools caused these men to expend a lot of energy. To replace this energy, the men consumed huge amounts of food. Breakfast usually consisted of eggs, bacon, sausage, and fried potatoes. Lunch had been prepared and set out for the men to take with them. A usual lunch included four sandwiches of lunch meat (beef or pork) and cake, cookies, and fruit. If they wanted more, extra sandwiches could be made by the men from the leftover bacon and eggs. The kitchen crew always had coffee available, and the men left their thermos bottles at the cook shack in the evening to be filled in the morning. Cutting crews left for the cutting areas by truck around 6:00 a.m. and worked until 4:00 or 5:00 p.m., with the skid and loading crews usually working for at least another hour.

Another marvelous meal awaited the loggers at dinner. It usually featured meat of some variety (fresh-killed deer or elk made the list from time to time) with potatoes, two vegetables, rolls, bread, cake, and cookies to top it off. The cooks prepared so much good food for these meals that in a period of five months, one commissary clerk ate so much he gained thirty pounds and could barely fit into his wedding suit. Each man in the camp paid for board with a whopping $1.05 per day deducted from his paycheck. This cost certainly had to be considered reasonable, for the food was all a man could eat. In the logging camps, meals of this order were a necessity rather than a luxury. Lumberjacks needed every calorie they could get.

The kitchen staff consisted of a cook, dishwasher, and two helpers who assisted with the cooking and serving. These men put in extremely long days, with their only breaks coming in the morning after breakfast cleanup and on Sunday when their duties required them to serve breakfast and only put out lunch meat for the rest of the day.

At Apex, lumberjacks used simple tools of the trade. The company provided each man with several crosscut saws and a double bit axe. A lumberjack had to supply his own wooden wedges for felling trees. The company also had a saw filer on the payroll who made daily rounds to sharpen the saws.

Skid crews moved the felled and bucked trees to the loading areas. Cutting crews bucked trees into sixteen-foot lengths in this district (other districts used thirty-six-foot lengths as their standard), and a choker setter placed a twelve-foot cable around the log and attached it to the skid cat or arch for dragging to the loading area. If the crew had a skid of less than a quarter of a mile, they attached the log to the cat, and if more, they attached it to the arch and raised the front end off of the ground to allow more ease of movement and less damage to the log. In later years, trucks came into use in some places to haul the logs to a loading area rather than lay more track or skid long distances.

Once at the loading area, loading and train crews took over handling of the logs. Tong hookers hooked up the log to the loader that then set it on the car. The Saginaw and Manistee Lumber Company owned the original cars used at the Grand Canyon District, which accommodated only one stack of sixteen-foot logs. In later years, longer cars leased from the Santa Fe held two stacks of sixteen-footers.

In order to take advantage of the type of loaders used on this district, the loggers cut sixteen-foot logs for delivery to the mill. The oil-fired steam loaders had small steel-flanged wheels that sat on tracks on the cars. The tracks came in two sections and were made to be picked up and laid down by the loader as it passed from car to car. As the loader-operator finished with one car, he backed the loader onto the section behind him, picked up the section in front, and swung it around to join with the one in the rear. Had it not been for this system, they would have used a stationary loader on skids that required the locomotive to move the cars into position for loading. By using this more efficient system, the crews no longer had the difficult chore of moving the skid loader to a new site.

Once loaded, the logs traveled to the siding at Apex for pickup by the Santa Fe and transport to the mill in Williams. When loads got backed up, they probably spotted log cars at Hopi siding, two miles south of Apex, for the Santa Fe pickup. The purpose of Hopi has never been clear, and this is the only possibility for its use other than as a doubling track. The Santa Fe logging extras brought empty cars from the mill daily and picked up the loaded cars for the trip south. These extras also positioned the cars for unloading at the millpond as a regular part of the trip. The mill crews rolled two or three logs at a time into the pond until they had emptied the car, then the train crew moved the next one into position.

The logging boss's job at Apex required him to act as the field general of the operation; he had a wide assortment of job skills to oversee. His position made him a salaried member of management, whereas the company paid the loggers hourly wages. Wages by today's stan-

Santa Fe double-length log cars in the Grand Canyon District.

dards seem exceptionally low, but the money bought more. For example, a choker setter made about 32¢ per hour; a tong hooker about 38¢; cat skinners made about 60¢; and the loader operator made about 65¢. Nothing to get rich on, but it was certainly a living wage during the Depression, when these men had a job and many others did not. But no matter what the salary amounted to, the company had a way to get at least some of it back.

The company maintained a commissary that sold tobacco, canned goods, soap, and some other household items. It was resupplied by truck from the commissary in Williams. As usual with company commissaries, they charged prices a bit higher than in the stores. The Saginaw and Manistee payroll department deducted commissary purchases from the men's wages along with board. Tusayan did not exist, and Moqui Camp, a place for tourists, did not stock groceries or merchandise, so shopping had to be done elsewhere. Occasionally the men drove to Williams or the Babbitt's store at Grand Canyon for their shopping needs. Thanks to the park service, the road to Williams had been paved, and except for the dirt roads from the camps to the highway, travel to town did not present a problem. At certain times of the year, the roads in the forest turn to mud. People in the camps did not consider it unusual to get stuck and spend the night in some abandoned buildings or whatever shelter could be found. During these times, the people used the commissary more frequently.

Cooks always kept a fresh supply of meat for the families. The company stored beef and other meats in a screened-in building open to the air. This served as the cooler. During the winter, spoilage did not present a problem, but they kept a minimum amount of meat in the summer. Trucks brought more in from Williams as needed. A housewife just went to the cook and purchased whatever cut of meat she needed for that day's meal.

Except for the location, family life in the camps could be compared with family life in Williams. Families that had school-age children usually lived in the headquarters camp at Apex, while those with preschool or no children moved with the advance camps. Quarters in the camps may have been smaller, but many families considered it more convenient to be closer to the work and the commissary car.

Organized entertainment in the camps did not exist. Some families visited each other for relaxation or made a trip to town. Mostly, they led a quiet life in the forest and oriented their days around the dictum "Early to bed and early to rise." Telephones provided the only reliable contact with the outside world. The Grand Canyon line had relatively good communications, with telephones at every station. Wires on insulators screwed into live trees ran from this line at Apex to the camps. The company

set out poles only where needed to cross large open meadows. These have all been removed, but insulators can still be found in many places today. The caller got the Williams operator to place the call and then disconnect when completed. Much of the time, poor connections across the country turned telephone calls into a shouting match, but in all probability the people at Apex had a phone system better than most.

Single men in the camps had little else but work and an occasional card or crap game to occupy their free time. For some, boredom could be relieved in Williams, but for most it just wasn't done, as many of the "single" men were not actually single at all. These men had families that in most instances lived quite far away and needed the money they earned. Swedes and others had left the old country to make enough money to bring their families over. Dust Bowl victims had been forced to leave their families with what was left of their homes while they searched for work. These separations placed additional strain on the men.

Some men observed an Okie Dust Bowler with his head in a rain barrel after receiving a letter informing him he had become a father for the first time. He emerged with a big smile, and someone asked him what he had done. "I was jes' listenin' to what 'Pappy, Pappy' sounded like," he replied. A hardworking Swede who had left his family behind presented an even sadder situation. Because of the separation, he had taken to drinking too much. While in the forest, he worked long, hard hours, saved his money, and stayed off booze. When he saved or borrowed enough to go to Sweden and bring his family back with him, he made the trip to Williams to catch the train east but couldn't pass up going into a bar. A few days later, he showed up back at camp, broke and hung over. This happened several times, and it is believed he never made it back to Sweden.

Fortunately, few serious illnesses and injuries happened during these years in the Grand Canyon District. With the nearest hospital in Williams and the nearest doctor only occasionally at the Grand Canyon, anyone seriously ill or injured had a long way to travel for medical attention. Any problem required that the stricken individual be placed in a car or truck and hauled to the nearest available treatment. Unless weather presented a problem, most people considered it easier and faster to take the patient to a doctor by vehicle because the scheduled trains on the Santa Fe ran only in the morning and evening.

When 1936 rolled around, the Saginaw and Manistee had nearly completed the timber-cutting leases in this district. Two U.S. Forest Service men stationed in the camps to mark trees for cutting and scaling (measuring them for board feet of lumber), finished up their work and went on to other duties. By May 1936, the last cuts had been made, and in June the final loads were left on the Santa Fe for the mill in Williams. With no more timber to be cut, the logging crews and families moved on to the next lease. This left only the maintenance men and the section gang to start the breakup of the camps and to pull the rail.

Santa Fe engineer Sid Terry with the Saginaw and Manistee 3 Spot at Apex in 1941. Salvagers cut up the locomotive for scrap at this location.

The rail remained in good condition, so they salvaged it for reuse or resale. Some of this rail might still be in service at the mines around Globe. All of the serviceable rolling stock and the living quarters that were still in good condition had to be packed up and sent on to the next lease area. Crews either scrapped or burned anything that had become unserviceable or was beginning to show its age. They rolled unserviceable log cars with wooden shacks on them into bonfires, one after the other. When the fires cooled down, the workmen picked up the leftover metal for sale as scrap. Classes continued in the school through the spring of 1936, and this caused it to be one of the last buildings to be moved. When all of the structures and equipment had either been dismantled or sent on to the next lease area, the hostlers parked the 3 and 4 Spot locomotives, never to be run again. They met the torch in 1941.

Today, all that remains of a living, vital community are rotting ties, wooden and stone foundations, rusted cans, an old stove, and other assorted pieces of history. Good memories also remain in the minds of those who once lived in a community with a unique lifestyle. It is a community to be proud of, for it brought together, in a very difficult time, the kinds of people who made this country great. Even now, it feels good to walk in these places and think of them.

Theodore Roosevelt during his visit to the North Rim and the Hopi and Navajo Reservations in 1913.

PRESIDENTS, KINGS, & WORLD CITIZENS
—PASSENGERS ALL—

WHEN THE PUBLIC LEARNED THAT the magnificent vistas of the Grand Canyon had been made accessible by comfortable rail transportation, they began to come in ever-increasing numbers. For many years, hearty writers who had visited the canyon when conditions were primitive extolled the beauty and unlimited vistas in newspapers around the country. Now, at the behest of the Santa Fe, these writers and others made the trip sound even more inviting. The railroad's passenger department also generated publications of its own to further advertise the line.

Dime novels had long lured easterners with stories of the Wild West that more than stretched the truth. When actual accounts of the Grand Canyon appeared side-by-side with these tales of derring-do, people had to come see for themselves. After all, wasn't Grand Canyon now civilized, with a railroad in place? With comfort insured, tourists ventured into the wilds of the Arizona Territory to see this wonder of nature. Oddly enough, many of today's travelers are looking for the same things. This is particularly true of foreign visitors, many of whom, thanks to television, believe cowboys and Indians still roam the West.

Those who were among the first to avail themselves of "civilized" railroad transportation got a little more than they bargained for. Stagecoaches remained part of the trip until September 1901. It was a dusty, rocking coach ride to the South Rim of the canyon from Anita Junction at first, and later from Coconino. It must have been worth it, because more and more came to enjoy nature's masterpiece.

In the years to follow, people in positions of power, such as presidents and kings, traveled the railroad right-of-way along with citizens of virtually every country on the planet. Many came in native costume, some dressed to the nines. All came away duly impressed. Some of the more famous tried to blend in, but for many this became an impossible task. Celebrities are usually too easily recognized, and world leaders have large security entourages. Others played to the press as if they were on the campaign trail. But no matter the status of the individual traveler, the Grand Canyon became a great equalizer. It could be no more or less spectacular to any of them. It is there and it is overwhelming.

Even John Muir, who had seen the grandeur of Yosemite and the majesty of Alaska, came away impressed. He had come expecting the worst from man's intrusion upon the scene. His trip in 1902 left him feeling awed by the beauty and expanse of the canyon and good about man's presence there. He returned several times, twice with Theodore Roosevelt. The two were old allies in the preservation of this country's natural resources. Both traveled by railroad.

President Theodore Roosevelt was the most ballyhooed visitor the canyon ever saw. At the height of his popularity, Teddy was a special favorite to Arizonans because of his Rough Rider regiment. Many of the Arizona men who served in Cuba with Roosevelt had returned to the state, and some even held high positions. All told stories that added to the Roosevelt legend. Publicity for his trip to the canyon appeared in the territorial newspapers for weeks prior to his visit. Along with the usual invitations to dignitaries of the Arizona Territory, members of the Rough Riders received special invitations for a reunion with their commander.

His visit to the Grand Canyon meant quite a bit to the people of Arizona. At stake was full-fledged statehood. Roosevelt was in favor of making Arizona a state, but other politics had to be played in Congress. Arizonans figured if they welcomed him energetically, he might be persuaded to make an effort with Congress. They pulled out all the stops. The Grand Canyon would

never see the likes of this visit, even when descended upon by 20,000 Boy Scouts.

Newspapers around the territory gave almost total coverage to the event. The *Coconino Sun* of Flagstaff printed the president's speech verbatim, and the Phoenix newspapers pretty much did the same. Apparently the editor of the *Williams News* was miffed when the president did not stop in Williams, Phoenix, Prescott, or Tucson. He printed a story that covered only a quarter column on page two, just to mention that Roosevelt had visited the canyon and been welcomed by several dignitaries. On page one, in an editorial, he belittled Roosevelt for not stopping. It made no difference to him that Phoenix and Prescott were far off the main line and Williams little more than a whistle-stop. You just can't please everyone!

The *Coconino Sun* devoted the entire front page of its May 9, 1903, issue to Roosevelt's first visit in Arizona.

PRESIDENT PASSES THROUGH FLAGSTAFF
Flagstaff's Patriotic People Follow Him in Goodly Number to Do Honor to the Nation's Chief Executive—President Presents Diplomas to Flagstaff High School Graduates—The Citizens of Flagstaff Present Beautiful and Costly Navajo Blanket

Wednesday morning [May 6] a large number of Flagstaffians gathered at the railroad station in order to be on hand to take advantage of the necessary stoppage for water, should Mr. Roosevelt arise so early, of catching a glimpse of the nation's well-loved chief magistrate, President Theodore Roosevelt.

At 4:03 a passenger engine drawing six Pullman coaches flashed by the station, seeming to frighten the shadows of the night which seemed adverse to giving way to the just-breaking dawn, back from the railroad into the settled portion of town, to come creeping back again when the engine had replenished its water supply and continued on its way....The train carrying the Presidential party continued on without material stoppage to Williams, thence over the Grand Canyon branch, arriving at Bright Angel at 9:30 a.m.

Excursionists from Flagstaff congregated about 5:00 a.m., and an hour later, at 6 o'clock, a train of five cars pulled out from this town bearing 301 enthusiastic people hot on the President's trail.

It was not the only special that day. One left from Phoenix "bearing nearly all the territorial officials" and another "carried the Cleveland Greys [sic], the crack military company of the country." The Grays traveled as the official escort of the president. About 200 people from Williams and a similar number from Prescott also came in on a special.

Mr. Roosevelt put in a full day. He had come to see the canyon, and see it he did. Someone placed a white horse at his disposal, and he made good use of it, riding along the South Rim. But he couldn't get away from the politicking. He made a speech about the virtues of the canyon and praised the railroad for not building anything on the brink. Most famously, he said, "What you can do is to keep it for your children, your children's children, and for all who come after you, as one of the great sights which every American if he can travel at all should see."

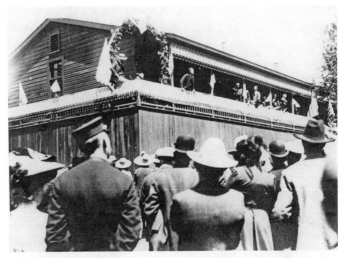

President Theodore Roosevelt addressing the crowd of people assembled at the Grand Canyon during his visit on May 6, 1903.

One boy and four girls, who made up the graduating class of Flagstaff High School, had a tale to tell. The president personally handed them their diplomas, and the territorial governor congratulated them. It didn't seem to matter to anyone that the students were "graduating" a month earlier than usual. For the ceremony, and to keep the crowds happy that festive day, the Arizona Lumber and Timber Company band made the trip from Flagstaff and played all day long.

The president left the next morning, but not before he determined this would not be his last trip to the canyon. He returned in 1911 and again in 1913, after he had stepped down from the presidency. No longer required to go through all of the hullabaloo on his subsequent visits, Roosevelt took some extended excursions into the canyon by mule. If nothing else, he became one

Theodore Roosevelt, John Hance, Emery Kolb, and party on the Bright Angel Trail in 1911.

of the canyon's most exuberant visitors and certainly one of its most ardent admirers.

Although statehood for Arizona would not come until February 14, 1912, Roosevelt continued to be welcome. The *Coconino Sun* of March 17, 1911, had the following two-column headline on the occasion of his next trip through:

> **FLAGSTAFF HEARTILY GREETS ROOSEVELT**
> **People Turn Out Several Hundred Strong to Greet Ex-President as He Passes Through Flagstaff—Remembers His Rough Riders**

Theodore Roosevelt may have appeared larger than life to many people, but President William Howard Taft, Roosevelt's handpicked successor, might actually rank as the largest dignitary to ride the rails to the canyon. At six foot two inches and 355 pounds, President Taft indeed cut an imposing figure. Stories of his bulk and oversized bathtubs were common. Shortly after taking office in 1909, he and members of his cabinet and staff embarked upon a rail odyssey that covered much of the United States. They traveled for nearly two months, from September 15 to November 10.

This inspection trip of the nation made for a magnificent adventure. It covered 12,759 miles in twenty-nine states and two territories (Arizona and New Mexico had not been admitted to the Union yet). They traveled mostly by rail on twenty-five separate railroads, although it was necessary to travel by steamer, ferry, and riverboat to visit certain areas. Taft's doubleheaded special to Grand Canyon came up from Phoenix via Prescott and Ash Fork. At Williams, on October 13 at

President William Howard Taft during his visit in 1909 as part of a marathon two-month survey of the United States that took him to twenty-nine states and two territories.

11:25 p.m., he stopped for a speech. Even at that late hour, the president drew a large crowd that wanted to hear about statehood. Taft did not disappoint them. Was he not Teddy Roosevelt's man? After the speech, he shook hands all around and then retired to his palatial private car. He left Territorial Governor Richard E. Sloan, Territorial Secretary George U. Young, and Territorial Representative Ralph Cameron to greet old friends and continue the assurances that statehood would someday be a reality.

Sometime after midnight, his train left for the canyon. According to the *Williams News*, "The old veteran engineers, Wagner and Lumsden piloted the special train of nine cars to the Canyon and back. Conductor Duncan was in charge of the train. Fireman Watts was on duty with Engineer Lumsden." They arrived at the rim early the morning of October 14. It is not recorded at what hour he arose to view the canyon. Because the speech at Williams had been one of 266 he made on this trip, and because of the late hour at which he gave it, it might be assumed he did not see the sun rise.

The canyon community had prepared for his arrival. Santa Fe crews laid new walks on El Tovar's grounds, and the dining room had been outfitted with new tables. Red, white, and blue bunting decorated the hotel inside and out. In addition, a group of twenty-five Indians had diligently practiced to "furnish amusement to the presidential party."

As with Roosevelt, the usual dignitaries made their obligatory appearance and many of the visitors who happened to be at the rim paid him attention. But there was no great outpouring to welcome him to the canyon as had been the case with Roosevelt. In two months' time, Taft saw and experienced more of this country than the vast majority of its people would in a lifetime. He could have easily bypassed the canyon, but he went miles out of his way to see it. Surely he was as impressed as have been the millions of people who followed him.

Taft's train left the Grand Canyon at about midnight on October 14. He departed as he had arrived—in the dark, seeing nothing of the sixty-four miles between the canyon and Williams.

In the years to come, the trip to the canyon by rail became an adventure for everyone who experienced it, whether they did so in 1901 or 1951. Anticipation of wonderful vistas made the trip an exciting experience: visitors knew what was to come even if they had never been there before.

Although the transfer from the main line to the Grand Canyon line changed in several ways over the years, it was always memorable. Usually passengers arrived at Williams on trains with fanciful names. The Scout, California Limited, El Capitan, Super Chief, El Tovar, and Grand Canyon Limited gave travelers a sense of impending adventure. Santa Fe crews spotted the Pullmans on the Grand Canyon track in Williams, making up the train for an early morning departure while the passengers slept.

Most Pullman passengers have the memory of being awakened by the porters at dawn. The sun coming over the high country of Arizona is a sight few people forget. Then came the mad dash to get washed, dressed, and ready for arrival at the canyon. Those travel-wise individuals who had been up the line before realized the urgency of making their morning preparations prior to entering the horseshoe turns of Coconino Wash; even the most seasoned travelers found it difficult to shave or brush their teeth while going through the curves. Besides, this fine scenery should not be missed.

For most years, Santa Fe timetables scheduled arrival at the Grand Canyon around 7:00 a.m. Easter Sunday was the only exception. Sunrise services took place at the Bright Angel overlook, and the train passed right by there. The agent, Sam Turner, had the train rescheduled until after the service had been completed and the choir finished singing.

This early arrival allowed everyone to reach the canyon in time for their first view before breakfast. The

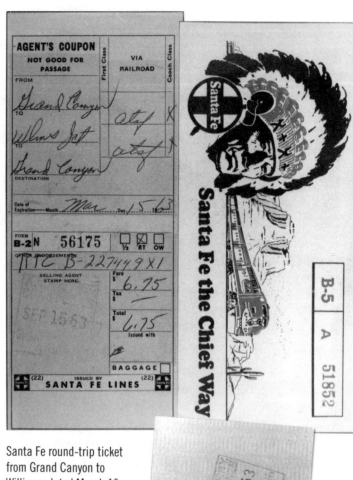

Santa Fe round-trip ticket from Grand Canyon to Williams dated March 15, 1963. **RIGHT:** Harvey Company one-way ticket from Grand Canyon to Williams dated August 9, 1963.

engine would pull trains as long as eighteen cars up the grade of the wye and then back down into the station. For a period of time, the Albuquerque Division Grand Canyon District timetable carried the notation, "No. 14 will turn on wye and back into Grand Canyon." Thankfully, no one took this literally. When the train stopped at the depot, the passengers stepped out into the crisp, rarified air of the rim's 7,000-foot elevation. Harvey buses waited to take them and their baggage to their hotel, with everything cared for without the passenger having to lift a finger. The first stop, right up the hill, was El Tovar. For many, this was their first sight of the canyon. As the bus pulled up and around the loop to the front door, the canyon dropped off to the right.

Such an immediate and unexpected introduction usually started, or stopped, people's hearts, as the case may be.

It did not matter if one stayed at expensive El Tovar or the more moderate Bright Angel Lodge, all passengers received the same treatment. Everything necessary was taken care of by the courteous, efficient Fred Harvey staff. Individuals could decide to do as much or as little as they wished. Fred Harvey buses left on trips to Desert View Watchtower and Hermits Rest on regular schedules. Drivers, well versed in the history and natural interpretation of the canyon, gave a tour that differed somewhat with the individual. Depending on which driver you had the fortune to be attached to, the canyon had been dug by Emery Kolb, "Captain" John

El Tovar's eight-car consist rests on Track 15 at the Grand Canyon with locomotive 3854 in the lead.

Locomotives 1370 and 3722 doubleheading the El Tovar past Bright Angel overlook at the Grand Canyon on June 15, 1941. El Tovar provided summer passenger service to the Grand Canyon in 1940, 1941, and 1946.

Hance, or Fred Harvey. The usual story about Fred Harvey was that he dug it trying to find a nickel he had dropped. Then there was the joke about the Chicago gangster who took one look at the great gorge, turned to his crony, and said, "Let's get out of here before they blame this on me!"

Railroad station staff kept busy all day long tending to the traveling needs of the passengers. Tickets were sold, telegrams sent, baggage handled, questions answered, and problems corrected. Agent Sam Turner always tried to anticipate the needs of passengers, especially those who looked a bit bewildered. One day, as he made his rounds up and down the station prior to the train's departure, he spotted an elderly lady who looked more lost than she should. In his most helpful voice, he asked, "Ma'am, where are you going?" The

reply was quick and direct. "Young man, that's none of your business!"

Sam was agent at the canyon for seventeen years. He and his wife, Eloise, were family to employees of the railroad, Fred Harvey, and the park service. He oversaw the physical plant and all the facilities built by the railroad while a Harvey man managed the hotels. In his capacity, many considered Sam to be the mayor of Grand Canyon Village, even if it was under the jurisdiction of the federal government. On March 20, 1957, Sam died of a heart attack in the Turners' apartment above the station, and he rests in the Grand Canyon cemetery.

After 1919, park service rangers always attended train arrivals and departures. They answered many of the same questions fielded by the railroad staff, with the same patience and courtesy. These men and women led interpretive walks and presented talks to visitors on

Sam Turner, agent at the Grand Canyon for many years, with his wife, Eloise, and son, Sam Jr., on the rim of the Grand Canyon in winter.

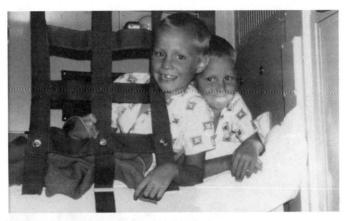

Two young passengers smile from their Pullman upper berth. A wake-up call at sunrise got them ready for the early morning arrival at Grand Canyon.

a variety of interesting canyon subjects. Many rangers held degrees in geology, biology, anthropology, archaeology, and other related subjects. Whatever their background, they introduced visitors to this wonderful place and educated them on its mysteries. Today, interpretive rangers are as much in demand as they were then.

Over the years, the railroad made several changes to Grand Canyon service. Schedule changes coincided with the main line trains. Santa Fe Trailways buses made runs to the canyon from Williams in the 1930s in order to accommodate passengers from trains that weren't transferring to the canyon line. They did so until the Harvey Company complained to the Santa Fe about the competition. After that, the Santa Fe dropped the service and Harvey buses made all of the normal transfers.

World War II brought on the most dramatic change in service. Railroad equipment was needed for the war effort. The War Production Board froze the develop-

ment of new locomotive design. Only proven models would be produced and time not wasted on developing new equipment. Travel for pleasure dropped off during the war, eliminating the Grand Canyon Railway's normal schedule, with the exception of the El Tovar and local trains.

On September 29, 1942, crew and station personnel lined up and posed for a photograph by Emery Kolb in front of the "Last Grand Canyon Train." The consist of one coach and a combination baggage/coach car behind engine 1800 was typical for the early war years, considering the light traffic. It was certainly not the last train, although it was the last to run on the regular Williams–Grand Canyon passenger schedule (trains 14 and 15) until the end of the war.

During the war, the Grand Canyon community became just another small town. Very few tourists traveled to the canyon; the only visitors in any numbers were Army Air Corps and field artillery soldiers from the desert camps in Arizona and California who used the Grand Canyon for rest and relaxation. Local civic organizations met in El Tovar, and ladies clubs kept busy knitting sweaters and scarves for the troops.

After the war finally ended in 1945, it took a while for the railroads to get back to normal. The heavy demands of the war effort had worn out their equipment. Troops still needed to be moved about the country, as several million men and women wanted to get home. And people were not yet in a frame of mind to do any recreational traveling.

On May 30, 1946, the Grand Canyon line opened back up for business. Now operating completely under the Santa Fe banner, two trains steamed into the yards at the Grand Canyon that day. One special carried Rotary Club members, and the local carried freight. Keeping with the custom for specials and the weekly local freight, both trains operated as extras. Timetables had not been made up for the Grand Canyon since 1942, and the line operated under the old schedule until the new one, published in September 1946, came into effect. On both, trains 14 and 15 made their return to the daily dispatchers' sheet. In addition, the local made the trip from Williams to the canyon for many years on Tuesdays, but that schedule changed to Wednesdays in 1959.

Specials, which were once big business, were back on track. Prior to the war, in the 1920s and 1930s, specials had been a way of life. For example, on June 3, 1922, twelve specials carrying Shriners and Rotarians strangled the yards at the canyon when they brought in 124 Pullman cars. In September 1938, eight specials for the American Legionnaires taxed the capacity of the yards. Including the local and two regularly scheduled trains, as many as eighteen special trains a day made their way either to or from the canyon, carrying Shriners, Rotarians, Boy Scouts, bankers, railroad societies, business groups, and organized tours.

Specials consisted of equipment from all over the country and Canada. Coaches and Pullmans from virtually every rail line might make up the consist. They looked a bit disorganized and certainly not uniform, but everyone considered them colorful.

There was little difference between the specials of the 1940s and 1950s and those that operated in the 1920s and 1930s. During June and July 1950, the Shriners, on their way to and from Los Angeles, stopped at the canyon in large numbers. On July 18, they matched the

Rose Bowl special coaches and Pullmans jam the yards at the Grand Canyon.

Specials filling the yards emphasize the last two curves of the Grand Canyon line. El Tovar is on the left.

Legion record of eight special trains. These trains all had doubleheaded steam for power. Rose Bowl teams made their appearance, as did their fans. The University of Michigan's team, band, and supporters brought two trains to the canyon in January 1951. Again, all steam. But the visit by the Boy Scouts of America in 1953 broke all records and became forever engraved in the minds of the people who happened to be there that July.

The Boy Scouts' annual Jamboree was held that year at Southern California's Irvine Ranch, and boys from every corner of the country passed right by the canyon on their way to the festivities. Scout leaders scheduled stops for all trains, even if only for a few hours.

Between July 12 and 15, the first contingents arrived en route to the Jamboree; July 25 to 28 saw the remain-

der on their way home. In these eight days, stopovers had been arranged for four to eight hours. Upwards of 20,000 scouts descended on the facilities like a plague—albeit a reasonably well-behaved plague. Souvenirs and sodas began to disappear at a phenomenal rate. The first stopover shocked the local population. They were better prepared for the second onslaught, selling everything in sight. Rangers patrolled the station, on the lookout for boys attempting to take home "natural souvenirs"

ılılılılılılılılılılılılılı
Five Shriner specials arrive at the canyon on March 28, 1937, with 1300, 3500, and 3700 class doubleheaded locomotives providing the power.

The Freedom Train, which ran after World War II to celebrate American liberty, visits the Grand Canyon on February 16, 1949.

line no longer had any block signals; they disappeared sometime in the 1930s. Communications workers and telegraph operators remember standing along the line at key stations to act as manual blocks. In this way, no train moved into a block until the one before it had cleared. The whole operation went off without a hitch.

In the late 1940s and 1950s, several international visitors made their appearance at the canyon. King Paul and Queen Frederica of Greece are the most well-remembered. "He was tall and good looking, and she was gentle," one resident commented. They arrived in four special cars for their stay. Dressed in everyday clothes, they visited all of the sights and then some. While on a tour around the village, the Queen asked to go into the school and speak to the children. Many still remember

such as ground squirrels and, in one case, a young fawn. These they returned to the wild.

During these visits, fifty-three specials, all with diesel power, brought in 669 Pullmans, coaches, troop kitchen cars (the army still had railroad transportation units in 1953 and had made these cars available), and dining cars. On July 28, equipment filled the yard to capacity when two sections of train 14 arrived along with seven scout specials: nine trains, 113 cars, two- and four-unit diesels! Not since 1922, when the Shriners and Rotarians brought in 124 cars, had the canyon seen anything like this.

These trains traveled with ten minutes between sections. With the yard full and visibility next to nothing, a system had to be devised to move these trains safely. For the first time at the canyon, Santa Fe personnel used radio communications to move sections in and out. The

King Paul and Queen Frederica of Greece with Superintendent Bryant in 1953.

Ranger naturalist Louis Schellbach explaining the topography of the Grand Canyon to the shah of Iran at a display in the Yavapai Museum with Superintendent Bryant looking on.

the day a real queen came to school, and one lady remembers being patted on the head by the royal hand.

Then came the day His Imperial Majesty Mohammad Reza Shah Pahlavi, shah of Iran, arrived. The shah viewed the canyon while dressed in a business suit. His entourage included many military men in uniform. Although he required tight security and seldom did anyone smile, Dr. Harold Bryant, the park superintendent, and ranger naturalist Louis Schellbach gave him the complete tour.

Dwight Eisenhower made a quiet visit in 1950 as the guest of Santa Fe president Fred Gurley in his private car. Not yet president of the United States, Eisenhower then held the position of president of Columbia University. He walked around quietly, talking with people and signing autographs. Ike made no fuss or demands, and

apparently enjoyed his visit.

Prince Faisal of Saudi Arabia and his retinue of sheikhs and bodyguards are one of the most startling groups to visit the canyon. Dressed for the most part in Arab costume, they presented a sight that caused many visitors to stop and stare. The Ethiopian bodyguards made the biggest impression. Large men by any standards, they were armed with scimitars encrusted with gold and jewels. One lady, invited to a tea for the prince at Dr. Bryant's home, asked to touch one of the swords and received a most definite but polite refusal.

One individual who later served as superintendent of Grand Canyon National Park remembers a wild ride as a boy in a jeep with the Saudis in their flowing robes. They used the jeep to travel around to the various overlooks. They only seemed to know the location of the accelerator and not the brake. This same young

Prince Faisal and Saudi Arabian sheikhs at one of the canyon overlooks during their visit in 1952.

Dwight D. Eisenhower at the east end of the Grand Canyon yards with
Santa Fe president Gurley's private car in 1950.

The Maharajah and Maharani of Kotah, a state in India, and their daughters during their visit in 1956.

Theodore Roosevelt made the most indelible mark. Grand Canyon lured him no less than three times, and these trips certainly helped to ensure the conservation of the natural scene. But he was not the only U.S. president named Roosevelt to make the trip to Arizona's Grand Canyon. His cousin, Franklin D. Roosevelt, and wife Eleanor visited the canyon before the start of World War II. He posed with railroad children, all the while flashing the famous Roosevelt smile.

Celebrities came to the canyon for relaxation and for work. Many movie, music, radio, and television personalities visited. Clark Gable, Edgar and Candice Bergen with Charlie McCarthy, Arturo Toscanini, Jimmy Durante, June Lockhart, and Doris Day are but a few. Actress Signe Hasse represented her native Sweden. Her comment on seeing the canyon for the first time was,

boy also got to ride in a tank during World War II. The tank belonged to a visiting army unit. Not everyone can boast of riding around the South Rim with Saudi princes and in an army tank.

The Maharajah and Maharani of Kotah, a state in India, arrived in 1956 along with the flamboyant President Sukarno from the Republic of Indonesia. Quietly, the maharajah and his family saw the sights and enjoyed the hospitality shown them by the park service. Sukarno, with his uniform and silver-capped swagger stick, stood out like a sore thumb. The village residents quickly noted his eager eye for the Harvey Girls.

Superintendent John McLaughlin gave King Mahendra of Nepal and his small group the usual VIP tour of the South Rim in 1960, when the king stopped over on his way from Washington.

Of the powerful people to visit the canyon, President

President Sukarno of the Republic of Indonesia at the rim in 1956.

"In Sweden our mountains go up!"

One of the more memorable celebrities was a heavy-set man who weighed too much to ride the Grand Canyon mules. Yet he captured the moods of the Grand Canyon and the pace of the mules on the Bright Angel Trail. Ferde Grofé wrote the magnificent *Grand Canyon Suite*. A gentle and very astute man, he had the ability to transform the sunrises, sunsets, and storms over Grand Canyon into beautiful music.

Television brought the canyon into the living rooms of millions of people. Dozens of documentaries have been filmed here. An episode of one television series was filmed at the rim: *Lassie*. Residents became extras, and the Hopi House magically "moved" to Indian Garden. Jon Provost, the young actor in the series, played with the canyon children when not involved in filming. A sudden snowstorm even provided the excuse for an impromptu snowball fight. Lassie presented a different situation. The filming schedule required four dogs to be available at all times. These gentle and well-mannered collies had to be kept groomed and clean. They resided in one of the Bright Angel cabins during their stay at the rim.

Residents of the village became avid television viewers in order to see themselves in their acting debut on the series. They saw themselves and neighbors transformed, just as familiar scenes changed names and locations to suit the script.

Tourists came and went. So did the powerful and the glamorous. Residents changed with the seasons and the years. Short and long trains arrived at the depot powered by steam or diesel. But the Grand Canyon of the Colorado was here before and remains. In comparison we, and our history, are here but a second.

President Franklin D. Roosevelt with the daughter of Grand Canyon Railway engineer Jack Tooker.

American Legion veterans and soldiers on convalescent leave at the canyon form an honor guard
during a memorial service for President Roosevelt after his death during World War II.

Locomotive No. 3853 rests on the Kaibab Formation in Tooker's Cut the day after the accident while supervisors try to decide how best to remove the wreckage.

ACCIDENTS

EOPLE WHO HAVE WORKED ON THE railroad have many good memories and stories. But occasionally, the stories describe the not-so-good times. Almost everyone who has built a career on the railroad in operations or maintenance-of-way remembers an accident.

When accidents occur, people are drawn to them like magnets. Railroad accidents can be especially spectacular, and many live on in song and legend. In fact, state and county fairs in the early 1900s made them into major events. Inside an arena, crews faced off, riding two obsolete locomotives on a length of track. They fired them up and started toward each other at full throttle. As soon as they got their hog rolling, the engineers jumped off. Then came the extraordinary sights and sounds: tearing metal, exploding steam, and spectacular damage. It gave spectators the thrill of a lifetime.

In these spectacles, there were no consequences for the audience: No terror, injury, or death. No cleanup of the torn equipment and track. No rebuilding or repair.

No expense for the destroyed material. Wrecks on a railroad, however, create complex situations involving many people, from the crew and passengers to the roadmasters, section gangs, equipment operators, doctors, nurses, administrative personnel, and lawyers.

Some accidents are simple, such as backing over a closed switch or breaking a knuckle coupler. Even these minor incidents require several people to report, investigate, repair, and remedy the situation.

The Grand Canyon line has been remarkably free from accidents compared to the main line. This is attributed to the different style of operations. Main line traffic moves at a higher rate of speed with a much greater volume and tonnage. At most, four scheduled trains a day made their way in each direction along the Grand Canyon road. Usually just one or two made the scheduled run. Some of these trains were extras, but at certain times and in certain years they became a regular part of the operations. As we saw in the last chapter, specials, sometimes in large numbers, made their appearance from time to time.

Occasionally, traffic on the line seemed heavy, but in reality it was not. The reduced speeds required by the many grades and curves also contributed to a lower accident rate. Maintenance of the road by the hardworking section gangs and bridge and building crews always kept the line in good condition. And except for the 4-8-4 heavy-weights, loads on the tracks never became as severe as those on the main line.

Atchison, Topeka and Santa Fe accident records for the Grand Canyon Railway prior to 1929 do not exist, therefore it's difficult to make a complete assessment of the accident trends of steam locomotives for this line. Only a partial comparison can be made of steam and diesel locomotives. Diesel operations are safer than steam for a variety of reasons.

The steam locomotive is a large, heavy, fire-breathing, steam and cinder–belching piece of machinery that gives the appearance of wanting to do harm. In reality, it is quite innocuous—until placed in the hands of man. Then it can be transformed into a people- and equipment-devouring monster.

Rail workers commonly got cinders in their eyes and burns from hot metal or steam. Slips from steps or grab irons caused scrapes and bruises, and sometimes more serious injuries. Only infrequently did equipment failure play a part in accidents and injuries. In the yards at Williams, a ruptured steam line blasted one hapless fireman from the cab of the locomotive. He received no burns but broke one leg in the fall.

Wreck of train No. 15 at Miller Wash on July 29, 1916. Locomotive 1256 rests on the bridge abutment that collapsed under its weight. Fireman Fred Terry lost his life in this accident.

Long and rigid locomotives obscured the vision of the hoghead when he needed a clear view the most. Because of his position, he might not always be able to see a hand signal given by a brakeman. This could result in backing over a closed switch or breaking a hose connection. The size, weight, and weight distribution of the locomotives also made them more prone to "getting on the ground" (derailed) by rolling rails on curves at high speeds. Flattened wheels, caused by locking the brakes and sliding the engine, commonly appeared in the accident reports. Broken couplers occurred when a hoghead put too heavy a hand on the throttle and didn't take the slack out slowly enough. Many things could go wrong with a steam locomotive, but they usually didn't happen until someone got careless.

Diesels have the same temperament when it comes to accidents—they're innocuous until the crew gets involved. But diesels create decidedly fewer possibilities for injury compared to steam power. Visibility is considerably better in a diesel locomotive because most units have a larger forward viewing area, and the engines are usually shorter and more flexible. Because of this greater visibility and the frequent use of radio communications, the brakemen and the engineer can communicate better. Cinders no longer plague crewmembers' eyes, but burns from hot engines happen from time to time. With a little ingenuity, crews still find ways to break hose connections and knuckles, back over closed switches,

and flatten a wheel or two. A moment's inattention also gives workers the opportunity to slip from steps or grab irons and ding their anatomy.

Diesels do have the uncontested edge on safety in the major accident category. There were no major derailments or deaths on the Grand Canyon line involving diesel equipment. Sadly, this is not the case for steam.

During construction of the line, a fair number of accidents probably occurred, but no reports of incidents have been found. If anything got on the ground at that time, it might have gone unreported just for good public and corporate relations.

The first known locomotive derailment cannot be documented with records, but the information comes

||||||||||||||||||||||||||||||
Wrecker and bridge and building crews clean up the damage caused by a washout that destroyed this bridge and abutments.

from a reliable source. This incident was not an accident. Two young brothers, looking for some mischief one summer day in 1902, found more than their share.

As they wandered near the yard limits on the north side of Williams, they threw an unlocked stub switch off the main line of the Grand Canyon road and then hid in the sunflowers, hoping to watch the returning train jam on the brakes and listen to the crew cuss. The trouble was, by the time the hoghead saw the open turnout, it was too late. Engine 282, the first scheduled locomotive to the canyon, went in the ditch and rolled over. While it lay there, belly-up with the bell ringing, the scared boys ran for home. Luckily, no one received any serious injuries, and probably some unknown brakeman got the blame for leaving the switch open. Apparently 282 did not sustain much damage, for it remained in service until 1905, when the Santa Fe sold it for scrap.

Two unusual points relate to this story. The boys never mentioned this story to anyone until after one had died and the other was close to finishing out his retirement from a long and illustrious career. That brings us to the other unusual point. For many years, he was senior engineer for the Santa Fe, and he ran the Super Chief through Williams. How many times did he wonder as he sped down the tracks, "Are there any boys out there leaving a switch open for me?" To the best of my knowledge, he finished his career on the Santa Fe with an admirable accident record and never went in the ditch.

Accidents along the Grand Canyon line started making the news soon after this one. The first of these, as well as the more serious ones, will be covered in this record.

According to the September 27, 1902, issue of the *Williams News*, the first fatality was caused by livestock. Cattle and sheep always presented a hazard along this line, and hardly a week went by without several being struck. In this instance, the consequences were far more serious.

WRECK ON CANYON RAILROAD
Work Train Derailed by a Band of Sheep— One Man Killed

A backing train, a cut on a curve with a heavy down grade, a large band of sheep and an excited herder resulted in a wrecked train, the loss of one life and a number of men being badly injured on the canyon railroad, about four miles north of Williams, last Saturday afternoon [September 20].

A work crew consisting of the foreman and eleven men had been waiting on a siding for the scheduled train to pass by. When they got under way, the caboose with all of the crew aboard backed the work train up the track toward their destination. Just before the accident, the train passed through a deep cut. When it came out of the cut onto a sharp curve, a large band of sheep under the charge of a Mexican herder began to cross the tracks and were confronted by the speeding train.

Conductor J. O. Dodge and brakeman E. S. McClure were in the cupola. One of the workmen hollered, "Look out! We are going to get into it." McClure applied the air in the caboose and Dodge signaled the engineer. Too late. The caboose plowed into the sheep, and as they piled up under the wheels, it derailed and rolled down the embankment, trapping the crew in or under the car. Fortunately, the locomotive remained on the tracks, allowing the engineer to beat a hasty return to Williams for help. Dr. Tyroler and workmen with tools boarded a car for the ride out to the wreck. The doctor treated almost all of the men aboard the wrecked caboose for injuries ranging from minor to serious.

One individual could not be helped. While the rest of the injured received medical attention, crews worked to retrieve the man's body from under the shattered caboose. After the injured had been given all of the treatment possible at the scene, they loaded them onboard the train for the return trip to Williams and further medical care. Their friend's body accompanied them on the journey to town. Follow-up stories reported the coroner's inquest, which levied no blame in the accident for the death of the workman, P. H. Swan, as the area is open range. The railroad returned Swan's body to his family home in Saint Louis in the company of a fireman from Winslow.

Newspaper stories reporting accidents did not seem to follow any particular format. The story above had a two-column headline, probably due to the unfortunate death of Mr. Swan. Editors banished accounts of other accidents of at least equal interest to the interior pages with no headline whatsoever. Witness the following story, from the September 27, 1903, issue of the *Williams News*, about a wreck in which an engineer was trapped for twelve hours under his locomotive. It was buried on the third page, along with advertisements and local stories of who was traveling where.

⎪⎪⎪⎪⎪⎪⎪⎪⎪⎪⎪⎪

No. 1256 in the ditch the day after the accident on September 23, 1903. Note how the bridge abutment collapsed under the weight of the locomotive and the track was displaced by the floodwaters.

Quite a serious wreck occurred about 9:30 Wednesday evening [September 23] on the Canyon road out near Anita. Heavy floods had washed away portions of the track and a special train pulled by Engineer Siegendaller ran into one of the washouts in the dark. The engine was overturned, pinning the engineer underneath, where he remained about twelve hours before he could be extricated. He was badly scalded and bruised up. Dr. Tyroler was summoned and went out from here on a special, but on account of the washouts on this side of the wreck he had to cover about eight miles on foot. Yesterday afternoon about four o'clock the delayed train arrived, bearing a large crowd of passengers and the injured engineer. His condition is not considered dangerous. The news of the washout was carried to Bright Angel—a distance of twenty miles—by a young man, one of the passengers, who reached there about four o'clock a.m.

That was the sum total of the story as reported. There was nothing further on the engineer or the young man who made a great effort in getting the news to the Grand Canyon. His trek of twenty miles in the dark, walking on a roadbed difficult to negotiate due to lack of ballast, surely should have received a bit more attention than that. Engineer Siegendaller probably appreciated his efforts more than anyone else.

Then in the issue of May 7, 1904, the *Williams News* reported the following story in two-column headlines.

WRECK ON CANYON ROAD
Regular Train Ditched Sunday by Broken Rail

Last Sunday [May 1] the regular Grand Canyon train was derailed a mile north of Valle, thirty miles from Williams. The accident was caused by a broken rail, and from the manner in which the engine, tender, two water cars and the combination baggage and smoking car bumped over the ties through a cut it is miraculous that no serious damage resulted and that no one was injured.

The accident happened, too, in the midst of the heavy traffic to the coast of easterners bound for Los Angeles to attend the Methodist conference, and a number of special trains were delayed many hours before the road was cleared.

The editor apparently decided the importance given a story based on his own priorities and how slow the news was that particular week. But usually, the news got short mention, like the following article in the February 4, 1905, issue: "About 3 a.m. Monday morning [January 30] train No. 14 on the Canyon road, ran over and killed twenty-seven sheep belonging to Charles Howard."

During the early years of the line, the terrible condition of the roadbed plagued the railroad constantly, and it is certain far more derailments occurred than made the newspaper. In actuality, the line was nothing more than a dirt track railroad with little or no ballasting. All of these accidents most likely became the moving force that got the railroad overhauled and literally rebuilt in 1907 and 1908.

The next two stories in the *Williams News* pointed to the terrible condition of the roadbed and the delays and inconvenience to passengers caused by the lack of sound tracks. Accounts of accidents suffered by a work train and a special point directly to the poor state of the right-of-way. Issues of March 4, 1905, and July 14, 1906, respectively, carried the following stories:

Last Sunday morning [February 26] Gallagher's work train on the Canyon road with Conductor Hogue in charge, went in the ditch at Twin Bridges, about twelve miles north of Williams. The tender, tie car, water car and commissary car were thrown from the track but no one was injured. The accident prevented the passenger train from getting through Sunday, but the passengers were transferred to a train sent out from here, and arrived some hours later. The roadbed is very soft from the recent storms, and although every precaution is being taken, accidents of this kind are liable to occur in spite of them. The track was repaired so as to allow trains to run on time Tuesday night but are not allowed to run on schedule time.

ELKS' TRAIN WRECKED

Last Wednesday afternoon [July 11] two special trains arrived here from Los Angeles, bearing the California delegation of Elks to Denver. The first section, leaving here at 3:30, was wrecked thirteen miles out on the Canyon road, the accident being due to the spreading of the rails. However, no one on the train was injured, though two of the Pullmans were derailed and some four hundred feet of the track torn up. The passengers were transferred to the regular train and taken on to the Canyon, where a banquet and a grand ball was held later in the El Tovar. All

other traffic was delayed till Thursday morning. The Elks returned to Williams that afternoon and continued on east.

Storms and poor construction by the original builders seemed to be the nemesis of the Grand Canyon line in the years before the Santa Fe decided to totally rebuild the right-of-way. Even after the overhaul, Mother Nature had a way of cancelling out all of the hard work. On July 29, 1916, tremendous thunderstorms delayed traffic on the line all day. A two-car passenger train at the canyon had been sitting out the storms for a couple of hours when engineer "Dutch" Oswald and fireman Fred Terry decided the time had come to give it a try. The *Williams News* on August 3 gave the following report:

Elks' special on the ground at milepost 13. The accident on July 11, 1906, was caused by the rails spreading when the roadbed got soft from heavy rains. Note the passenger coaches passing on the shoofly and the extra water car on the special.

CLOUD-BURST CAUSES CANYON ROAD WRECK
Fireman Fred Terry Loses His Life— 4000 Feet of Track Washed Out

As the evening train on the Canyon road was making the run from Grand Canyon to Williams last Saturday night it ran into a flood between Anita and Willaha which had been caused by a cloud-burst. The speed of the train was slackened and engineer W. E. Oswald felt his way along, but on reaching and entering upon a bridge over Red Horse Wash the engine went down taking engineer Oswald with it and fastening fireman Fred Terry between engine and tender. Engineer Oswald escaped from the wreck without serious injury but before fireman Terry could be released he was enveloped in steam from a bursting pipe and scalded to death.

The storm deposited tons of rain and hail in the drainage that crossed under the railroad. When floodwaters reached the bridges spanning the wash, hail began to pile up around the abutments and pilings and formed a dam. Backed-up water flowed over the tracks and around the bridges. Ballast and tracks washed away along with several bridges. When engineer Oswald eased out onto the bridge, the abutments no longer had the strength to support the weight of the locomotive, and it came crashing down.

Several follow-up articles appeared with eulogies for Fred Terry and accounts of his funeral. Out of consideration for the family, the *News* did not report that Terry's last hours had been long and painful. Consequently, nothing could be reported about how much Oswald had tried to help Terry. Oswald lost several toes to frostbite from standing for many hours in the hail while he attempted to comfort Terry. The fireman did die before a doctor arrived, and the crew packed his body in some of the hail piled up around the bridge to keep it in better condition. Another unusual part of the story also never made print. Prior to leaving the Grand Canyon, Terry told Oswald he had a premonition about that night. He said, "I know I'm gonna get it tonight."

Another problem with this story is that the location given was incorrect. In several official and news accounts, Red Horse Wash, which is between Anita and Willaha, was given as the location. Actually, the accident occurred four miles farther south, at Miller Wash. This is two miles south of Willaha and north of Valle. Santa Fe engineering drawings put the location of the accident at bridge C-36 (now D-36), which today is right at milepost 36. For some reason, train and track crews still carry on the misnomer and refer to this as Red Horse Canyon.

In 1916, the line curved heavily through Miller Wash, with four bridges spanning the turns of the creek. These curves necessitated a considerable reduction of speed even in good weather, and today the signboard restricts speed through the wash to twenty-five or twenty miles per hour (twenty-five for freight and twenty for passenger). After a realignment in 1931, the line through the wash became relatively straight, with only one curve between the third and fourth bridges. This straightening of the line caused the milepost to be moved about a half mile north from where it was at the time of the accident.

With the curves in place at the time, the speed restrictions, and the weather conditions, engineer Oswald must have been driving the train at a crawl. And yet the momentum of the train was sufficient to carry it over the washed-out abutment onto the partially washed-out roadbed. His slow speed is indicated by looking at the photograph of the scene and noting very little damage to the combination car, which literally dropped into the creek with very little forward momentum.

It appears engineer Oswald had taken reasonable care under the circumstances. Certainly he cannot be faulted for not realizing the potential a major thunderstorm cell holds for disaster. Who would believe such an incredible amount of hail and water could be concentrated in one small drainage? Who would believe that the amount of hail necessary to form a dam could be deposited in such a short period of time? An ice dam at bridge C-36 caused the south abutment of the bridge to wash out when the water piled up behind the dam at the spans and flowed over the fill at the abutment.

Although news reports changed the location, they did give a reasonably accurate account of the damage to the roadbed and bridges. Santa Fe field engineers made the impressive final tally. The flood moved 1,000 feet of track six to ten feet off the fill and washed out all of the ballast from milepost 36 to bridge C-36, a distance of 4,000 feet. Furthermore, the tons of water and ice shifted one of the three bridges out of line and completely destroyed the other two.

Passengers suffered little injury but had to be returned to the canyon until the following Monday. A train delivered them to the accident site, and transportation around the gap brought them to another train, which carried them to Williams. The accident at Miller Wash brought out the best in many people. Everyone did their best, from engineer Oswald to the hardworking crews who literally rebuilt one mile of track and three bridges in one week.

An automobile accident at a crossing turned out to be one of the more unusual along the line. It involved the Santa Fe doctor from Williams. The following headline appeared in the January 15, 1926, *Williams News*:

GEORGE BARNES KILLED AND DR. MELICK SERIOUSLY INJURED IN RAILROAD CROSSING ACCIDENT
George L. Barnes Was Killed Almost Instantly and Doctor Melick Was Seriously Injured Thursday Morning [January 14] When the Inclosed [sic] Car in Which the Men Were Riding Was Struck by Southbound Grand Canyon Train at Abra Crossing, Formerly Known as Valle

Dr. P. A. Melick, Santa Fe physician and surgeon, in his office in Williams about 1900. Dr. Melick survived a railroad crossing accident at Valle in which his passenger, George Barnes, died in 1926.

Williams hospital built by Dr. Melick in 1898 in which he treat railroad and local patients for many years before and after his accident.

An early morning rabbit-hunting trip had lured Barnes and Melick to the Cataract Creek country west of Valle. The crossing at Valle station made for the quickest and best way to the "Island" country. With Dr. Melick's Maxwell closed up to the cold, they approached the crossing from along the stockyards and never heard or saw the train until it was too late. George Barnes saw the train first. He yelled, "Train, Doc!" and attempted to jump, but the train hit them before he could get clear. When the engine hit the car, the right side caved in, and this is what saved Dr. Melick's life. Barnes, thrown from the vehicle, came to rest in a rock pile. The crew found Melick near a telegraph pole with the car on top of him. Directly above him, the bashed-in side of the car protected him from further injury.

Because of the obstruction posed by the stockyards,

neither the car's occupants nor the locomotive crew saw the other until the car arrived on the tracks about 100 feet in front of the train. Impact occurred even before the brakes could be applied. When the train finally stopped, the trainmen raced back to the crossing. Barnes could not be helped, but the crew removed Melick from under the wrecked car and treated him as best they could. The trainmen loaded Barnes's body and Dr. Melick into the baggage car and brought them into Williams.

Later newspaper articles eulogized George Barnes and gave accounts of Dr. Melick's progress. He did remain unconscious for about two weeks after the accident but survived and regained most of his mobility. Melick never completely recovered from the injuries he suffered in the accident, but he did return to his medical practice and lived to help many of his fellow Williams residents.

A veteran conductor for the Santa Fe who worked on both passenger and log trains did not fare as well. He met his fate while working on the log trains he preferred over passenger service. On June 20, 1935, Harlie M. Goss fell to his death as his train passed in front of the Fray Marcos Hotel. The account of the accident appeared in the June 21 issue of the *Williams News*.

TRAGIC DEATH MEETS RAILROADER

Harley [*sic*] M. Goss, 51 year old pioneer Northern Arizona Railroad conductor, was instantly killed at 4:45 o'clock Thursday afternoon when he fell into the path of the slow moving log train. The wheels passed over one leg through the pelvic bone and hip, bringing instant death.

Delivery of log cars to the Saginaw and Manistee millpond on the southwest side of town necessitated backing the train down to their siding. The locomotive pushed the train from the rear with Goss occupying his usual position at the front of the lead log car. When the car had reached a position in front of the ticket office, witnesses observed Goss climbing up on the logs in an apparent attempt to signal the engineer. He fell from the top of the log stack, but no one could determine

Log train wreck in 1916 with conductor Harlie M. Goss standing on top of the uppermost log. **LEFT:** Conductor Harlie M. Goss in his Santa Fe passenger uniform about 1929. Goss died when he fell under the wheels of his log train in 1935.

the reason. The witnesses reported seeing him "straighten up and then throw his arms upward and fall."

Goss became the last person to suffer a fatal accident on the Grand Canyon line. He had survived the Spanish-American War and several derailments in the past but did not escape from this one. It is thought he suffered a heart attack, causing his fall. The people of Williams and the Grand Canyon held him in high regard, and eulogies gave glowing accounts of his history and contributions to those communities and the railroad.

One last major accident waited in the wings. On July 27, 1939, a special entered Tooker's Cut at the north end of Coconino Wash a bit too fast for the curve and got on the ground. Actually, it got on the wall. The August 3 issue of the *Williams News* carried the following account:

Trainmen pose with wrecked log train near the Saginaw and Manistee mill on July 30, 1916. A broken rail caused the wreck.

WRECKAGE CLEARED, SERVICE RESUMED ON G. C. RAILWAY

At eight o'clock last Thursday night a special Santa Fe passenger train carrying tourists from the Grand Canyon was wrecked in a "cut" about eight miles south of that city on the Grand Canyon Railway. The train was a double-header and the two engines left the rails on a curve in the cut, lodging up against the solid stone embankment on the outside of the curve. The combination baggage and bar car followed the engines and lodged against the embankment, but the car behind it broke loose, turned at right angles to the track leaped the embankment and took out across country for several yards before it came to a halt still standing on its wheels. The next coach followed after the engines while the rest of the train remained on the tracks.

Another special, following about ten minutes behind, could have plowed into the wreckage even with the reportedly brilliant moonlight, as there had been no time to set out warning flares. The hoghead (whose name did not appear in the reports) averted what could have been a real tragedy when he saw the rising steam and recognized it for what it represented. Had the boilers been punctured as reported, there probably would have been an explosion with loss of life. Actually, the rising steam came from ruptured cylinders that had been broken open on the limestone wall.

Reports told of engineer Sparks, despite his own severe injuries, refusing to leave the accident site until all passengers had been accounted for, calmed, and given first aid. Fifty-one people had been injured, five seriously. Ambulances took the people with serious injuries to the Grand Canyon, and the remainder boarded the other special for the return trip.

The accident occurred at a rather difficult location. To clear it required a wrecker from Winslow and another from Needles. Maintenance-of-way supervisors made original estimates of several days to a week for removal of the wreckage and track restoration, but crews working furiously cleared the tracks and in three days, scheduled service resumed. Not including transportation costs, lost revenues, medical expenses, and settlements from lawsuits, the cost to the Santa Fe for damage and repairs amounted to $51,701.74. The Williams station became a madhouse the day after the accident when a fleet of forty Fred Harvey and Santa Fe Trailways buses brought all

Santa Fe wrecker from Needles preparing to lift No. 3853 back onto the rails on July 28, 1939. Crews did a remarkable job of clearing this wreck in three days.

of the passengers from the two specials into town. The baggage had to be brought in on another fleet of rented trucks, as the buses did not have enough room.

Nothing is ever simple or glamorous about railroad accidents, but they are certainly spectacular, and occasionally, the memory brings a bit of a chuckle.

When one of the heavy 2900s got on the ground at the Grand Canyon, roadmaster M. E. Spivey arrived to find the crew and the section gang all awaiting his instructions. To add to his problems, he had an audience of Santa Fe management giving him and the engineer advice on how to get the locomotive back on the track. Spivey had considerable experience with this situation and went about his business.

He put his section gang to work lining up spare track, ties, tie plates, and frogs to his satisfaction while ignoring the interruptions of the "armchair" management. After getting everything set, he told everyone to back off and went to talk to the engineer. He asked, "Who's the boss here?" The hoghead came back with a direct, "You are, Mr. Spivey." "Good!" he said, "just remember that and pay no attention to those other people over there," referring to the management men. "Just put the power to her and keep her going until I tell you to stop."

Spivey had orchestrated this concert. He took the position of maestro at the podium and raised his arms. The engineer sat poised with his hand on the throttle of his 975,400-pound instrument. Critics in the form of Santa Fe brass awaited their chance to offer unwanted advice or to say, "I told you so" in order to show their superiority. Swinging his arm, Spivey gave the engineer the highball and the concert was on! Immediately, tie

A case of backing the train too far in the Grand Canyon yards.

plates and ties began to fly in all directions as the tremendous weight of the 2900 and its tender brought to bear 66,000 pounds of tractive force from the drivers. The brass began to scream and holler for the engineer to stop, but he kept on with Spivey giving him the go-ahead. In a matter of a few seconds, the huge locomotive sat on the tracks in fine condition. With only the light panting sounds of the steam passing through the valves, the locomotive gave the impression of a huge puppy quite pleased with itself. The only casualties were the red-faced brass. When a concert is well planned and orchestrated, the music is sweet.

Coal-burning Atlantic and Pacific 4-6-0 ten-wheeler in the Williams yards.
It later became the Atchison, Topeka and Santa Fe 429 class No. 433.

STEAM AND DIESEL
—The Power—

ISTORY, TRADITION, SCENIC RIDES and a sense of nostalgia for things past attract people to railroads. But when asked to single out a reason for their interest, the overwhelming answer is the locomotives. It's probably because of the raw power they exude, even as they stand still. Rhythmic pumping and gentle hissing of steam give rise to the feeling that a steam locomotive is breathing. Earth-shaking rumbles from a parked diesel give the impression of a wild animal waiting to charge. When first approached, a locomotive does not seem like a large inert piece of machinery but rather something alive that a person can get to know and become attached to. Power has a way of attracting people. When people can harness and control that power, it becomes even more attractive.

Steam and diesel locomotives have their proponents, and both deceive the casual observer. Hardly anything appears more complex than a steam locomotive. Yet it operates under simple principles. It is intricately constructed, but the technology is straightforward. Diesels appear to be quite simple as well, but in reality, they are quite complex. Imagine being the master of something as complex or intricate as a locomotive. Design and operation of such a wonder is beyond the dreams of most people. But to know that other human beings build and operate them is a heady thought.

Locomotives in motion epitomize power, control, and grace. They always seem to do as they wish, pleasing everyone without opposition. Once you've experienced the sight and sounds of a steam locomotive, especially a doubleheader working up a grade under a heavy load, you'll never forget it. Billows of smoke and steam, the sound of bells, whistles, and the thrilling barkin' of a locomotive in full cutoff are the essence of memories. To uninitiated souls, these sounds could be disconcerting. The early morning trains pulled into the wye at Grand Canyon Village, chuffin' and clanging up the grade near the tourist cabins. It was not unusual to see a half-awake tourist in his shorts come running out the door of his cabin in a state of mild panic as the

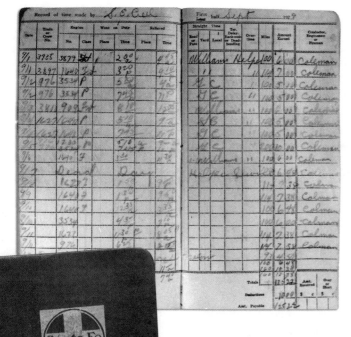

LEFT: Pages from fireman S. E. Creel's time book dated September 1929. Note Grand Canyon (GC) entries. **BELOW:** Cover of engineer E. L. Schmitz's Santa Fe Rulebook No. 43438.

Village was home to many of the crew. Children and wives would be waiting for Father to come home on the morning train.

Every now and then, something a little out of the ordinary gave these family members something to look forward to. One morning, a conductor's daughter waited to greet her father, as usual, along the tail of the wye. As she strained her eyes, looking for her dad, she glanced into the cab of the locomotive. Her father was running it! The hoghead, who wore a wooden leg, was nowhere to be seen. When her father stopped the train at the station and climbed down from the cab, the excited daughter lit into him with a barrage of questions: Why are you running the train? Where is the engineer? To all of this, he calmly replied, "He got his leg waterlogged." The fireman just stood there and grinned.

Crews started their day at one or two in the afternoon, when they got out of bed and got something to eat. This left a few hours until check-in, and they either spent the time with their families or watching the tourists. Mule passengers in the corrals and on the trail provided the most entertainment. Dudes showed up wearing shorts and all sorts of unsuitable clothing to ride the mules into the canyon. Wranglers patiently sent them back to their rooms after advising them of the improprieties of their choice.

Most of these dudes had never seen a mule, much less been on one. Almost all of the riders did not have any idea what to expect, for they had never had the op-

locomotive came a barkin' up the wye. Having arrived the night before, he probably wasn't even aware there were any railroad tracks within miles of the place. He should have been up at the rim watching the sunrise anyway.

Many people in the village looked forward to train arrivals in the morning. As the train backed down the wye, the laundry staff usually waved it in. After a two-hour and fifteen-minute pull-up, the road crew looked forward to this daily greeting. Grand Canyon portunity to become accustomed to the ways of mules. The ladies' embarrassment always provided some fun when the mules did what came naturally just after starting down the trail. The mules have a regular relief station, and the first mule always made his stop. Riders screamed and hollered all they wished, but the mule didn't budge until he was finished. Some passengers asked the wranglers to make the mule stop doing what had to be done. Much to the further embarrassment of the rider, they replied, "Lady, he's doin' jes what you had to do this mornin'." Bad enough for the first rider, but the others in line knew what was going to happen next. Some passengers even dismounted and walked away until their mount had taken care of business.

After the train pulled into the wye in the morning, it backed into the station for the passengers to off-load. Service personnel cleaned the cars (car attendants at Williams did the major cleanup during the night) and performed minor maintenance. Hostlers serviced the engine and filled the tender at the Poage water column. The Santa Fe never built or even authorized an engine shed at the canyon. For all of those years, hostlers serviced the locomotives in the open with no shelter from the weather. Hostlers and mechanics completed major servicing and maintenance at the roundhouse in Williams. After servicing the locomotive, the hostlers then coupled it to the train and left it to wait for the crew. Steam pressure in the boiler needed to be kept up while the train waited for the return run to Williams. The hostler did this by attaching a steam line from the powerhouse to the locomotive and keeping a low fire in the firebox.

When the crew arrived for the evening train, the usu-al paperwork needed to be filled out, train orders issued and signed for, and equipment inspected. The conductor signed the forms, inspected the cars, and got ready to receive the passengers. Hogheads and firemen made sure the motive power had been serviced and they had all of the required safety gear. The brakeman checked the trucks, brakes, air and steam connections, and couplers on the cars.

To begin his inspection, the fireman climbed up on the tender and checked for a full load of water. He then measured the fuel with a dipstick. The lubricators for the water pump always required a thorough examination. Regulations required certain equipment to be carried at all times. The fireman inventoried these items: two tallow pots of valve oil and engine oil (kept above the firebox to keep them warm), all safety gear such as fusees, torpedoes, the red-and-white lantern, lit and ready, and a spare bucket of antifoam compound for the water. He made sure the sand box contained enough

The railroad and people of Grand Canyon Village had strong ties to the old Santa Fe steam locomotive bell, and even today the high school uses it as their victory bell.

for the run and the scoop. Then he went up on top to oil the bell and back into the cab to inspect the firebox for carbon buildup. Too much carbon got a hostler in trouble, as his job required him to get it raked out. Last but not least, he checked the water glass (to make sure there were spares), steam pressure, and the injectors.

The hoghead gave the whole locomotive a good going over to make sure everything worked properly. He checked the cylinders and air pumps for leaks and function, and then lubricated everything in sight that moved. The engineer needed the old long-stemmed oilcan to reach the valve guides, pony trucks, butt ends, and the brakes on the tender and drivers. Then he climbed up into the cab to check his valves, injectors, and controls. Satisfied that all was well, he kicked back and talked with passengers who looked over the engine and asked all sorts of questions about what made it go and why.

Crew and station personnel line up for a photo with locomotive 1251, a 1226 class 4-6-2 Pacific with three coaches and a combination car, at the Grand Canyon Depot about 1915. Note the trees between the tracks.

Making it go is no real problem. Knowing how to make a locomotive do what you want it to do when you want it to do it is another story entirely. The fireman's job is to provide the steam. The engineer's job is to use it. Together they get the train to its destination.

Some hogheads delighted in giving their firemen a rough time. With the Johnson bar in the corner and the throttle wide open, a fireman had all he could do to keep water hot, much less keep up enough steam. Between exhortations of "Smoke 'er, laddy!" and "Kid, you haven't got enough hot water over there to boil eggs in!" the sweat- and dirt-streaked fireman would be bustin' his chops.

Firemen, especially on the Grand Canyon line, have a real problem keeping water at the correct levels and maintaining the right amount of steam pressure. Keeping track of how much water is in the boiler while going up and down grades is a real skill. While going uphill, the water glass is full, and downhill it is empty. Somehow, with up to twenty-five or thirty valves above the boiler head, injectors, fuel preheaters, and airflow through the firebox door, temperatures have to be kept up and water levels maintained. Water must be kept above the crown sheet in the boiler or it becomes superheated. If this happens, water can slosh over the sheet, and with the instantaneous burst of steam generated, the boiler will explode. While going uphill with a low water level, the flue

||||||||||||||||||||||||
Fireman Frank Merrifield uses the Poage water column at Grand Canyon to fill the tender before the return run to Williams. The water column was located on the north side of the yards near the old powerhouse.

tubes can be exposed with the same resulting burst of steam blowing off the front of the locomotive. On an uphill run, if there is too much water in the boiler it will flow out of the whistle. Water flowing out of the whistle is no great problem, but when too much water is in the boiler it will be forced into the cylinders and cannot be compressed as steam can. Water in the cylinders means a loss of power and must be blown out.

A standing rule exists for low water problems: Stop the locomotive as quickly as possible without sloshing the water. Cut off the fuel flow and get away from the engine until it cools down. Good reasoning!

Firemen lived by the glass and died by the glass. It tells how much water is in the boiler and what to do. Usually, the glass is maintained at one-half to three-quarters full. The fireman has to be able to read it accurately, even with grade changes, power changes, and braking. If the glass breaks, it's replaced while en route. A broken water glass in the winter means a cab full of steam and no way to see until the valve is turned off.

Fuel is controlled by the fireman as he tries to maintain optimum temperatures. All locomotives on the Grand Canyon line, except during the turn of the twentieth century, have been oil fired. Some required preheated oil and others cooler oil. Oil is forced into the firebox under a jet of steam with two valves controlling the flow. One is for the fuel and the other is for the atomizer. Temperatures are controlled by direct and indirect water lines below the cab that adjust the fuel temperature before it gets to the firing nozzle. These procedures determine how fine a mixture is sent into the firebox and how far it is thrown forward before burning. Thus the firing rate is adjusted to match the work

The weekly local arrives at the canyon in a snowstorm. Crew members prepare to switch No. 830, a 2-8-0 825 class engine, onto the wye.

being done by the engine.

Harassed firemen seldom had any recourse to the occasional hoghead who overworked and cussed them out for being too slow or doing the wrong thing. One did have his day, though. After a particularly bad run with the Johnson bar in the corner, the throttle wide open, and the hoghead constantly on his back about what a rotten job he was doing, one fireman had had enough. As the train pulled into Williams just about out of water, fuel, and steam pressure, the fireman grabbed his bag and slid down the ladder. The hoghead hollered, "Where do you think you're goin'?" To which the fireman replied, "If you're so damn smart about running this engine and firing it too, I'm gonna see how you do it by yourself 'cause I'm goin' home!" And he did!

To become a hoghead requires being a fireman first.

Maybe some of them remembered how hard they had worked and the abuse they took on the job from other hogheads. Probably they just passed it on. Others remembered the abuse they received on the way up and treated their firemen with respect and consideration. At any rate, firing is quite a responsible position, particularly on varnish (passenger) runs. Years of being a fireman and getting to know the equipment, being able to pass the examinations, and waiting for an engineer to move or die could make a man a bit coarse around the edges.

Examinations for engineers are quite comprehensive. They had to be, particularly on the Grand Canyon line. Nowhere else in the Santa Fe system was an engineer faced with such abrupt changes in grade and curves. Many of the curves are at the ten-degree maximum. Horizons are deceiving; it's difficult at times to determine if you are going uphill or down. This line is so demanding that the Santa Fe filmed it for use in a Link simulator designed to train engineers. It has been said that if an engineer can run the Grand Canyon line, he can run anywhere on the Santa Fe.

Questions on the examinations covered machinery and air extensively. Engineers had to know everything about the several brake valves and how to put the steam on one side if necessary to bring in a disabled engine. Rule book questions had to be answered exactly. Santa Fe exams always asked about Rule G. It pertained to the use of liquor, and rails commonly paraphrased it: "Thou shalt not haul more than thy tonnage." Another question is sort of obvious. "What is the first thing you do after leaving the station?" Answer: "Look back to see if the train is following."

Hogheads running steam have their own assortment

1226 class 4-6-2 Pacific No. 1227, ready for a Grand Canyon run at the Williams roundhouse.

of valves and levers to control. They can assist the fireman with water problems by using the injectors on the engineer's side (the right side) of the cab. Their controls are primarily the Johnson bar, throttle, reverse lever, and the air for the brakes.

Putting the Johnson bar "in the corner" provides full power. It changes the travel of the valve with respect to the piston, except when the reverse lever is on center. In effect, this is the neutral position. On center with the reverse lever allows just a slight movement of the valve. Forward or reverse position allows further travel and more steam worked in the cylinder. As speed builds, the bar is notched back a bit to keep back pressure from

developing. The throttle, through a system of valves, meters the amount of steam from the boiler to the cylinders. As the engineer pulls out on the throttle lever, linkage lifts up the throttle valve in the steam dome and steam enters the dry pipe, which takes it to the steam chest and then through valves into the cylinders. If the engine is equipped with superheaters, the dry pipe takes the steam to the superheater header, which sends it through the heater units, back to the header, and into the steam chest. When the engineer uses the throttle and

Johnson bar properly, the steam is used efficiently and provides the most power for the amount of fuel burned.

Air, or the brakes, and its use or misuse has been the subject of many slang terms for engineers. An "air man" is generally considered to be better than average at handling the brakes. Good control of the brakes is imperative, particularly with the 3800 class locomotives, which had notoriously poor brakes. After looking back to see if the train is following, a good hoghead then gets the feel of his train by testing the air. With all of the grades and curves in the next sixty-four miles, he has to know when to apply air. For these two and

a half hours, he is in full-cutoff, drifting, braking, and half-throttle situations.

Speed is a constant consideration. Grades and curves on this line frequently reduce speeds to fifteen and twenty miles per hour. Most steam locomotives didn't have speedometers, so the hoghead sat there with watch in hand, counting rail joints, telegraph poles, or mileposts in order to figure his speed. Later, the larger locomotives

1337 class 4-6-2 Pacific No. 1370 and 3700 class 4-8-2 Mountain No. 3722 wait in front of El Tovar Hotel for the return trip to Los Angeles at the head of the El Tovar on June 15, 1941.

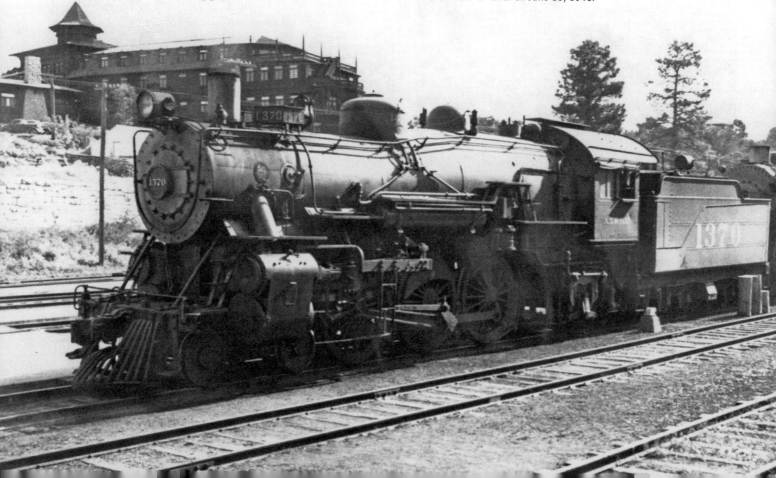

came equipped with speedometers.

Before the days of two-way radios, doubleheaders presented another problem. The engineers in the lead cab and the helper could not communicate. Each had to get a feel for his engine and the other. The lead handled the air by regulation. He was also responsible for taking out the slack and getting the train moving. The helper had to know when to add power and slack off. Power was added by the helper after the lead, but it had to be eased off prior to the lead. They controlled power to maintain speed and drift as required in order to conserve water and fuel. If they worked together properly, they didn't have to make a water stop.

The cabs of steam locomotives are noisy, hot, and dirty while running. Cinders from the stack of the early coal burners or from the volcanic ballast always had a

3500 class 4-6-2 Pacific 3500 class 4-6-2 Pacific No. 3520 leaving the Grand Canyon yard limits with train No. 11. **ABOVE:** 3160 class 2-8-2 Mikado No. 3234 at the engine-servicing area just below Bright Angel Lodge.

way of finding an open eye. Locomotives of the 1600 class rode really rough, and the larger 4-8-4s much more smoothly. Trips to and from the canyon became a routine: do this here, do that there, and watch out for cattle and sheep. Many runs hit something, especially at night. Usually they collided with one or two steers at a time or as many as twenty-some sheep. Sheep were the most dreaded. Wool gets tangled in the running gear, and the stomach contents are sprayed up into the cab. It is a real mess to clean up. Even worse, sheep can derail a train easier.

But the real obstacle is a large bull. Hitting one of these is an experience unlike any other. Because of the size, there is more to be spread all over the cab. One hoghead who was known to be a joker and loved to tell a story had occasion to initiate a new fireman one evening. As the train came up on a bull in the middle of the tracks, he told the fireman to put his head outside to make sure the bull cleared the track after being hit. Following orders, the youthful fireman didn't notice the hoghead closing his window. The bull's remains spread all over the cab. Afterward, the fireman said, "I wore that cow!" He knew better the next time, but the hoghead had another story to tell.

One might wonder why the hogheads didn't stop the train instead of hitting the livestock. Usually it is too late after seeing the livestock to make a sudden stop without risking injury to passengers. A hoghead trailing varnish has as his first concern the safety of passengers. Better that the railroad pay for dead stock than injure the unsuspecting people who rely on the engineer for safe passage.

Hogheads have a tendency to be cantankerous. Maybe it's the years of working hard and taking abuse as a fireman before becoming an engineer or the long hours that make them this way. Whatever it is, there are lots of good times to help temper their lives and make being a hoghead something to be proud of.

One hoghead in particular was always cantankerous. Early one morning, as usual, he headed into the Harvey House in Williams for breakfast. The Harvey Girl serving customers at the counter was having a bad day too. When he ordered his pancakes, she returned with the oversized stack on a smaller plate. The hoghead made it plain that he wanted a regular-sized plate so he could pour syrup over them. The Harvey Girl, in a roundabout, earthy way, told him he wasn't going to get another plate. Our hoghead then proceeded to put the cakes on the spotless counter, pour syrup on them, and finish his breakfast. He didn't even leave a tip when he left.

Trains were the focus of life in Grand Canyon Village for many years. Both the gleaming luxury liners of stainless steel and the ordinary coaches in railroad green attracted tourists and villagers. But the big attraction of the railroad has always been the pulling power—the locomotives.

There have been at least forty-one classes of steam locomotives, from the venerable old 4-6-0 and 4-4-0s to the magnificent heavyweights of the 4-8-4 classes that serviced this line from its inception until 1953. Engine number 3893, a 2-10-2 of the 3800 Santa Fe class, probably became the last steam locomotive to make this run, in 1953.

It is always interesting to watch a steam locomotive, but it's especially thrilling given the size and power of the larger 4-8-4s and 2-10-2s. Engines of the 3800 class were the largest single group of the 2-10-2s to run the line. Those of the 900, 1600, and 1674 classes were also

3776 class 4-8-4 Northern No. 3780 poses for her factory photograph.

used extensively. The 3800s weighed in as the lightest of the heavyweights at a maximum of 710,500 pounds, but they had a great tractive force of 75,000 to 85,000 pounds. Ten drivers gave a distinct advantage to these locomotives on the grades of the canyon line. However, engineers had their hands full running them on the 112 curves of up to ten degrees radius.

Some of the most impressive locomotives for size, the 3751, 3765, and 3776 classes of the 4-8-4 variety, looked massive. They made up the next-to-heaviest classes, ranging from 808,946 to 960,630 pounds. Easy to drive and comfortable to ride, their crews appreciated these hogs over most others. However, with only 65,000 to 66,000 pounds of tractive force for all of that weight, they were not the most efficient locomotives for this line. They fared much better on the main lines, where they could use their speed to advantage.

Eastbound Santa Fe Grand Canyon with 3765 class 4-8-4 Northern No. 3775 in the lead passes a freight in the hole at Cajon Pass.
ABOVE: 3700 class 4-8-2 Mountain No. 3748 rests between runs on the engine-servicing track at Grand Canyon.

PHOTO GALLERY

William Diehl

Grand Canyon Railway steam locomotive 4960, formerly of the Chicago, Burlington and Quincy Railroad, heads across the sage flats between Williams and the Grand Canyon.

LEFT: Dozens of bridges span the uneven terrain along the Grand Canyon line, requiring constant upkeep from bridge and building crews.

BELOW: Lookout Studio (upper left) is perched on the South Rim between Yavapai and Maricopa Points, the perfect spot to showcase expansive views of Grand Canyon.

Originally built for the Lake Superior and Ishpeming Railroad, steam locomotive 18, seen here as it exits Grand Canyon Village, was one of three vintage engines purchased for the Grand Canyon Railway in 1989.

Christopher Muller

OPPOSITE TOP: One of the first buildings Grand Canyon Railway passengers will encounter as they pull to a stop in Grand Canyon Village is the stately El Tovar Hotel, built by the Santa Fe Railroad in 1905 just steps from the historic Grand Canyon Depot.
OPPOSITE BOTTOM LEFT: Mikado 4960 steams through northern Arizona's ponderosa pine forest.
OPPOSITE BOTTOM RIGHT: All aboard! Diesel engine 237 pulling historic rail cars awaits its passengers at the Williams Depot.

ABOVE: As the train leaves Williams, the scenery changes with the elevation. Soon ponderosa pine forest is replaced by high desert dotted with cliffrose, chamiza, and big sagebrush.

William Diehl

Xanterra Parks & Resorts

ABOVE: Billowing steam contrasts with a snowy scene midwinter.
LEFT: A steam engine passes a siding en route to the canyon.

William Diehl

Locomotive 29 hauled iron ore in Michigan's Upper Peninsula when it worked the Lake Superior and Ishpeming line in the first half of the twentieth century. A century later, this mighty engine still experiences snowy winter days, now on the Colorado Plateau.

A steam and diesel doubleheader snakes through hilly terrain.

The Grand Canyon Railway's observation dome cars and luxury parlor car make for a memorable ride.

Xanterra Parks & Resorts

Diesel engines 237 and 239, built in 1977, were used by Amtrak until the 1990s. Grand Canyon Railway purchased them in 2004 and completely refurbished them before putting them back into service.

The setting sun fills Grand Canyon with brilliant color.

Diesel engines first made their appearance at Grand Canyon in 1938, but did not come into regular service until the early 1950s. Today, three EMD F-40PH diesel locomotives pulling beautifully restored rail cars are the primary motive power for the Grand Canyon Railway.

Xanterra Parks & Resorts

Xanterra Parks & Resorts

Train conductors manage the activities of crew and oversee the loading and unloading of cargo. In addition, conductors check passenger tickets, announce stations, and help passengers as needed.

Every winter, the Polar Express comes to life, taking children and their families on a moonlit ride from Williams to Santa's Village, where the jolly old elf climbs aboard.

Xanterra Parks & Resorts

Xanterra Parks & Resorts

Strolling cowboy musicians and the Great Train Robbery entertain passengers on their way to the canyon.

Xanterra Parks & Resorts

Xanterra Parks & Resorts

The Grand Canyon Depot, built by the Santa Fe Railroad in 1910,
is the only rail station in a national park. El Tovar Hotel, completed the
same year, stands sentinel behind it, on the rim of the canyon.

At 975,400 pounds, the 2900 class 4-8-4s certainly became the heaviest class to ply the line. This was the last steam locomotive class purchased by the Santa Fe and saw only limited use on the canyon line. They appeared nearly identical to the other 4-8-4s, and like them, the tractive force of the 2900s left something to be desired. They could only produce 66,000 pounds of tractive effort for all of that weight.

Of the 311 steam locomotives identified to date as having run on the Grand Canyon line, only four are still in existence. Number 2913 is beautifully preserved in a park next to the Mississippi River in Fort Madison, Iowa. Its cousin, 2926, sat quietly in a park in Albuquerque, New Mexico, for many years until the dedicated New Mexico Steam Locomotive Railroad Historical Society began its restoration. The state fairgrounds in Topeka, Kansas, is the final home of the high-wheeled 3463. Those not being returned to service receive periodic care to preserve and maintain them for public observation. High fences surround these locomotives and keep them distant from those who would otherwise like to personally experience the size and beauty of these mechanical marvels.

The fourth is also an exception. Number 3751 has been restored to operational service by the San Bernardino Railroad Historical Society. Starting in 1986, this nonprofit group of dedicated steam devotees rescued 3751 from a park in San Bernardino and has since waged a constant battle for funds to rebuild, maintain, and return this class locomotive to the rails she once ranged. Evidence of their success came in the form of 3751 re-creating the heyday of steam power by heading up a passenger special from Los Angeles to the Grand Canyon for the 2002 National Railway Historical Society annual convention.

No matter if the equipment is a light- or heavyweight,

|||||||||||||||||||||||||||
3880 class 2-10-2 Santa Fe No. 3859 rests with another 3800 on the engine-servicing track below Bright Angel Lodge.

there is nothing like steam power, and it is at least interesting if not thrilling to watch in operation. But in February 1938, something new arrived on the Grand Canyon scene. During a snowstorm on February 10, diesel unit 822 of the 2 class pulled into the depot at the head of the Santa Fe Chief on its maiden voyage from Los Angeles to Chicago. The demonstrator unit sported the livery of the Electro-Motive Corporation, as it did not belong to the Atchison, Topeka and Santa Fe.

Hot on its heels, on February 18 diesel unit 6 of the 2 class made its first appearance at the head of El Capitan. Also arriving in a snowstorm, it made a more spectacular contrast to the white snow thanks to the bright red, yellow, and silver colors of the new Santa Fe Warbonnet livery. On its first Los Angeles to Chicago run, El Capitan made a grand entry to the canyon. Rated at 1800 horsepower, the single unit number 6 trailed five stainless steel cars built by Budd Company. This train stayed over on the nineteenth and left the morning of the twentieth.

Neither of these trains ever appeared on the Grand Canyon line schedule. Both came in as extras strictly for the publicity. The Grand Canyon became the plum of Santa Fe's advertising department, and it made the most of these two stops. Santa Fe was an innovator with the introduction of diesel power to railroading, but diesels did not become a part of the regular schedule to the Grand Canyon for another thirteen years.

Regularly scheduled diesels first came to the canyon

Fireman Leo Black and engineer Jim Maule on the pilot of 4000 class 2-8-2 Mikado No. 4095 at the canyon after a run in the winter of 1948.

in 1951. In September, engineer Ray Bartee and fireman Leo Black brought the first unit in as a lead engine. The actual date and the number of the unit have been lost to time. An interesting note is that the day before, they made a test run to see if the diesel could handle the grades of this line. It came in behind a steam locomotive for insurance.

Steam continued to run regularly on the Grand Canyon line even with the introduction of diesels in 1951. Diesels filled out the schedule 100 percent for the first time in February and March of 1952.

Did the engineers fight the changeover? Not on your life! As one said, "Hogheads fought to get on the diesels. They were a damn sight easier on the eyes, ears, and life than those dirty, noisy, stinkin' steam engines." But do they miss the steam? You bet your life they do!

Engineers and Santa Fe management all waited to see how the diesels performed on the 3 percent grades along the line. Steam stalled down at maximum capacity, and at first so did the diesels. The underpowered early diesels also had a tendency to burn up the electric traction motors when overloaded. But they proved to be the better engine as power improved. Diesels are less prone to slip on the slick tracks of the grades during frost or rain because of their lower gear ratio, more uniform distribution of sand, and the flexibility of the trucks.

Diesel locomotives only have four to six axle trucks and smaller wheels as compared to the many different

2900 class 4-8-4 Northern No. 2926 resting in an Albuquerque, New Mexico, park. These locomotives weighed in at 975,000 pounds and were the largest to run on the Grand Canyon line. Cousin No. 2913 rests in a park next to the Mississippi River in Fort Madison, Iowa. Both ran doubleheaded to the canyon. No. 2926 is being revived and will return to service.

sizes and configurations of trucks and the large drivers of the steam locomotives. This gave them a distinct advantage on the grades and curves of the Grand Canyon line. Steam engines have one to two axle pony trucks in the lead just to guide the longer and heavier locomotives into the curves. Drivers are larger, not geared, and they cover a longer, less flexible distance than the diesels do. Trailing trucks number from none in the smaller engines to one or two axles in the larger engines just to carry the weight behind the drivers. On this line, one steam locomotive could have as many as sixteen wheels compared to the diesel's eight to twelve.

When the diesels came into regular use, the hogheads and firemen faced an unusual problem. The Santa Fe had no training program to teach the crews how to run them. The hoghead had to learn by watching others and asking questions as he rode in the cab. About every six

months, Electro-Motive Corporation sent an instruction car around to do a show-and-tell on the brake systems. That was about it until later years, when the railroad put Link simulators into service. Even the engineers' exam continued to ask a majority of questions on steam for many years after the introduction of diesels. There were no questions on troubleshooting at all, and only a few on the air brakes—curious procedures for a company that turned out safety brochures and posters by the ton.

As with steam locomotives, diesels are built for specific jobs, but most have been used for other assignments than those for which they were classed. They are classed for passenger, freight, passenger/freight, and as road switchers. It was not uncommon to see all types represented in the canyon yards.

Early units came in multiple sets. For instance, the 2 class engines only had the L (lead) unit, while 16, 37, 100, and 200 class diesels came in L, A, B, and C units. The 300 and 325 classes had L, A, and B units, and 52 class engines had L and A units. These sets did not remain complete throughout their service, either. Units 22A, 24B, and 32C could have been coupled with 18L. This is why you will not see complete sets in the power roster for diesels.

It is worth noting a couple of unusual types that ran this line. In the 700 class diesels, numbers 726 through 731 used specially built (by Santa Fe) steam-generating tenders to provide steam for the passenger cars. They converted six truck tenders and fitted them with a turbine and two boilers each. The Santa Fe painted numbers 9000 through 9004 on the sides in the standard font.

The Atchison, Topeka and Santa Fe used 2650 class

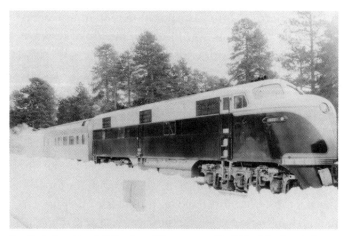

The first diesel to visit the Grand Canyon was No. 822 at the head of the inaugural diesel consist of the Santa Fe Chief in 1938. This 2 class engine belonged to EMC and served as their demonstrator.

diesels of the road switcher variety for several years along the line. Although of the same class, individual units differed in that 2651 through 2654 came equipped with a steam generator to handle the passenger cars and others with dynamic brakes. The dynamic brakes were new to the Grand Canyon line at the time these locomotives came on the scene. Dynamic brakes employ an electrical means to convert some of the momentum into heat, thereby providing a retarding force within certain upper and lower speed limits. The GP series (Geep) presently operated by the Grand Canyon Railway originally is of this class and style but has been completely rebuilt by Santa Fe. The most obvious difference is that the high nose of the early versions has been removed for better visibility.

Steam locomotives have been modified and reconfigured for years. Some were simpled (from compound to single cylinders), and others had their wheel arrangement changed to suit them for a new job (main line to switching). Early model diesels also went through rebuildings; older F-7s came out as new road switchers, and 1100 class engines went through rebuilding and came out as 3100 class. The major modifications usually resulted in power increases, style, and livery changes.

With the introduction of diesel locomotives, firemen have gone through the greatest changes, with little or nothing for them to do in the eyes of the railroads. On most railroads today, the position of fireman no longer exists. The "featherbedding" issue was a long and bitter fight between the railroads and the unions, and won't be covered here. However, firemen are still with us and remain a part of the progression to engineer on the Grand Canyon line.

When diesels made their appearance on Santa Fe locomotive rosters, firemen rejoiced. Among other more comfortable aspects, they no longer had to sand flues nor contend with freezing temperatures when the firebox door needed to be opened in the winter for more draft. But firemen found other uncomfortable duties waiting for them in early diesels. Each power unit had two fans and four shutters that had to be adjusted manually. The fireman went outside on the units and made these adjustments as needed. Eventually, even these duties went by the wayside, and the firemen became observers and engineer trainees.

Gone also, except for their rare appearance on a scenic line, are the days of doubleheaders and two crews. Now, one engineer handles all of the units from his position in the lead unit. Communications with other crew members are handled by radio, which is more

effective and provides less room for error. The old ways might have been romantic, but there are better ways to do things sometimes.

Steam power is one of those things that lurk in the mind's eye and occupy a favorable memory. No matter that it is "dirty, noisy, and stinkin' steam," the mastery of such equipment always evokes pride in one's work. The hoghead doesn't exist who can't find something good to say about steam if he had the opportunity to work with it. The newer breed of diesel engineers also speak well of their equipment, and they will remember the "good old days" in years to come. There is good

TOP: The second diesel to arrive at the canyon provided a bit more color. No. 6, also a 2 class engine, sported Santa Fe's new Warbonnet livery on the inaugural run of El Capitan. **ABOVE:** 300 class F-7 No. 303 three-unit diesel locomotive.

and bad with all things, and people have the tendency to remember those things that give them pleasure. Like the conductor, reading a bill of lading for a sheep stock loader to Quivero and asking the hoghead, "What the hell are E-WEs?" The word was "ewes"—female sheep.

325 class F-7 No. 338 three-unit diesel saw limited service on the Grand Canyon line.

1200 class GP-30 Nos. 1211 and 1214. Engines of this class ran in regular service on the line.

F-7s and a GP-7 tend to trains stacked up in the yards at Grand Canyon.

1300 class GP-35 No. 1314 diesel locomotive. GP-35s ran regularly on the Grand Canyon line in the 1950s and '60s.

Boy Scout specials jam the Grand Canyon yards in 1953. 2650 class GP-7s and 300 class F-7s head up the specials.

MOTIVE POWER ROSTER FOR THE GRAND CANYON RAILWAY

This roster of steam and diesel locomotives that plied the Grand Canyon line has been compiled from photographs, accident reports, train sheets, train orders, logbooks, telegrams, newspaper articles, and personal interviews.

— STEAM —

[All manufactured by Baldwin unless otherwise noted]

CLASS	TYPE	NUMBER
	4-8-0	SFP 19 (Rhode Island)
	4-6-0	SFP 49, 51
	4-6-0	SFP 70 (Pittsburgh)
	4-4-0	SFP 88 (New York)
23	4-4-0	33 (Schenectady)
41	4-4-0	45, 49 (Schenectady)
125	4-4-0	125 (New York)
281	4-6-0	281, 282
354	4-6-0	370 (Pittsburgh)
468	4-6-0	470, 475, 485, 486, 495 (Rhode Island)
566	2-6-0	610
631	4-8-0	637 (Rhode Island)
649	2-8-0	649
664	2-8-0	678
709	2-8-0	722 (Dickson)
769	2-8-0	782 (Richmond)
789	2-8-0	791, 795, 806, 809, 811, 812
825	2-8-0	830, 833, 836, 840
900	2-10-2	907, 909, 911, 923, 942, 947, 948, 953, 954, 955, 956, 958, 959, 960, 963, 964, 965, 968, 976, 978, 979, 984
1226	4-6-2	1227, 1229, 1230, 1235, 1239, 1241, 1242, 1251, 1252, 1256, 1258
1270	4-6-2	1272
1309	4-6-2	1309, 1322, 1331, 1332, 1333, 1334
1337	4-6-2	1337, 1338, 1339, 1340, 1341, 1342, 1343, 1364, 1367, 1368, 1369, 1370, 1371, 1372, 1373, 1376, 1378, 1379
1600	2-10-2	1620, 1623, 1624, 1627, 1628, 1629, 1630, 1632, 1633, 1634, 1638, 1640, 1653, 1659, 1663, 1665, 1669, 1672, 1673
1674	2-10-2	1675, 1676, 1677, 1680, 1681, 1682, 1683, 1684, 1685, 1687, 1689, 1690, 1691, 1692
1800	2-6-2	1800, 1812, 1816, 1823, 1827, 1833, 1839, 1844, 1850, 1859, 1886
1950	2-8-0	1959, 1960, 1961, 1963, 1965, 1966, 1967, 1968, 1970, 1971, 1972, 1985, 1990
2160	4-6-0	2173
2900	4-8-4	2913, 2917, 2926
3100	2-8-2	3119
3129	2-8-2	3136, 3139, 3142, 3143, 3151, 3152, 3153, 3154, 3155
3160	2-8-2	3210, 3229, 3230, 3234, 3238, 3240, 3241, 3243, 3254, 3256
3450	4-6-4	3456
3460	4-6-4	3463, 3465
3500	4-6-2	3520, 3521, 3522, 3524, 3525, 3526, 3529, 3531, 3532, 3534
3700	4-8-2	3701, 3703, 3704, 3705, 3706, 3707, 3708, 3710, 3711, 3721, 3722, 3726, 3727, 3728, 3731, 3734, 3735, 3736, 3737, 3738, 3739, 3740, 3741, 3742,

			3743, 3744, 3745, 3746, 3747, 3748, 3749, 3750
3751	4-8-4		3751, 3753, 3754, 3755, 3756, 3758, 3760, 3761, 3763, 3764
3765	4-8-4		3767, 3768, 3770, 3771, 3772, 3774
3776	4-8-4		3777, 3780, 3781, 3784, 3785
3800	2-10-2		3807, 3818, 3833, 3837, 3939, 3850, 3851, 3852, 3853, 3854, 3855, 3856, 3857, 3858, 3859, 3860, 3861, 3862, 3863, 3864, 3865, 3866, 3867, 3876, 3877, 3878, 3879, 3880, 3881, 3882, 3884, 3885, 3887, 3888, 3891, 3892, 3893, 3894, 3895, 3897, 3898, 3899, 3900, 3901, 3902, 3903, 3904, 3905, 3906, 3907, 3909, 3910, 3911, 3912, 3913, 3914, 3915, 3925, 3927, 3931, 3932, 3933, 3934, 3935, 3936, 3937, 3938, 3939, 3940
4000	2-8-2		4005, 4007, 4010, 4013, 4014, 4033, 4036, 4059

Possible other classes utilized: 507, 1290, 1452, and 5000.

—DIESEL—

[All manufactured by EMD* unless otherwise noted]

CLASS	MODEL	TYPE	NUMBER
2	E-2	A1A-A1A	6, 822 (EMC*)
16	F-3	B-B	16L, 17L, 18A, 18L, 19L, 22A, 22C, 22L, 24A, 27C, 28L, 30A, 30B, 31A, 32A, 32B, 32C, 33L, 34A, 35L
37	F-7	B-B	37A, 38A, 38L, 39C, 41L, 42A, 44A, 44L, 45C
52	PA-2	A1A-A1A	54A, 57L, 76L (AlCo*)
100	FTA/B	B-B	155, 415
200	F-7	B-B	250L, 254L, 257L, 259L, 263L, 273L
300	F-7	B-B	302L, 307L, 310L, 312A, 312B, 313B, 313L, 314A
325	F-7	B-B	325L, 328L, 328A, 329L, 329A, 334A, 340L, 363L, 415L (these became Amtrak power)
700	GP-9	B-B	717, 726, 727, 728, 729, 730, 731, 735, 744, 746, 747 (726–731 used steam generator tenders 9000–9004)
1200	GP-30	B-B	1201, 1208, 1210, 1216, 1221, 1223, 1225, 1226, 1232, 1234, 1235, 1241, 1243, 1244, 1246, 1248, 1251, 1254, 1257, 1260, 1262, 1263, 1264, 1266, 1267, 1269, 1270, 1274, 1277, 1278, 1279, 1280, 1282
1300	GP-35	B-B	1300, 1302, 1303, 1304, 1305, 1315, 1317, 1333, 1334, 1337, 1338, 1339, 1340, 1342, 1346, 1348, 1350, 1352, 1357, 1359, 1367, 1369, 1370, 1373, 1377, 1378, 1385, 1387, 1388, 1390, 1391, 1394, 1395, 1401, 1404, 1405, 1408, 1409, 1410, 1413, 1418, 1419, 1420, 1425, 1437, 1439, 1440, 1456

2650	GP-7	B-B	2651, 2653, 2654, 2659, 2692
3100	GP-20	B-B	3151
3200	GP-30	B-B	3210, 3211, 3212, 3236, 3238, 3239, 3241, 3244, 3245, 3250, 3251, 3254, 3269, 3270, 3274, 3280, 3282
3300	GP-35	B-B	3309, 3317, 3337, 3340, 3342, 3349, 3352, 3370, 3372, 3388, 3390, 3397, 3402, 3409, 3410, 3411, 3416, 3424, 3432, 3439, 3441, 3442, 3444, 3447, 3448, 3451, 3453, 3460

*EMD—Electro-Motive Division of General Motors Corporation
*EMC—Electro-Motive Corporation
*ALCo—American Locomotive Company

MOTIVE POWER ROSTER, 1989–2016

— GRAND CANYON RAILWAY STEAM —

CLASS	TYPE	NUMBER
SC-3	2-8-0	29 (Former LS&I)
SC-4	2-8-0	18, 19, 20 (Former LS&I)
O-1A	2-8-2	4960 (Former CB&Q)

— GRAND CANYON RAILWAY DIESEL —

MODEL	TYPE	NUMBER
GP-7	B-B	2072, 2134 (Former AT&SF)
FPA-4	B-B	6762, 6773, 6776, 6788, 6793 (Former CN)
FPB-4	B-B	6860, 6871 (Former CN)
F-40PH	B-B	237, 239, 295, 4124, 4128
GP-7u	B-B	1105 (Former AT&SF)

— FOREIGN DIESEL —

LINE	MODEL	TYPE	NUMBER
A&C	GP-9	B-B	3802
Amtrak	P-32BWH	B-B	503, 505, 507, 508, 509, 512, 514
	F-40PH	B-B	217, 231, 291, 305, 315, 334, 358, 364, 369, 373, 393, 406
	P40B	B-B	815, 816, 818, 822, 823, 830, 831
	P42B	B-B	1, 4, 7, 20, 25, 30, 31, 34, 36, 45, 46, 48, 53, 68, 72, 74, 80, 88, 93
AT&SF	FP-45	C-C	100, 101 (Now BNSF 90, 91)
	GP-30	B-B	2713, 2728, 2769
	8-40BW	B-B	520, 559
	SD40-2	C-C	5111
	SDF40-2	C-C	5259
BNSF	9-44CW	C-C	1039, 5403
Siemens	Sprinter	B-B	RS1
WS	E-9A	A1A-A1A	10A, 10C

Flanders Auto 20 Pathfinder touring car stopped by the rim, 1920.

MUST ALL GOOD THINGS COME TO AN END?

PPARENTLY, THE SAYING "ALL GOOD things must come to an end" does not apply to the Grand Canyon Railway. There have been times, particularly in 1942 and 1968, when people believed the Grand Canyon line had, come to its natural end. Throughout the 1970s and '80s, most believed this railroad would never carry passengers again. On September 17, 1989, that all changed.

Nothing remains exactly the same as when it began. Things change, and that is the natural order. Historically, the Grand Canyon line has followed this rule from the day she was born in the minds of the men who brought her into being. The Santa Fe and Grand Canyon Railroad became the Grand Canyon Railway, followed by the Grand Canyon branch of the Atchison, Topeka and Santa Fe Railway, which was eventually partially owned by Railroad Resources, Inc. The rule is still being applied, as the railroad is now owned and operated by a new company called the Grand Canyon Railway. After an infusion of $15 million and a lot of hard work, the company began operations on the eighty-eighth anniversary of the original passenger run to the canyon.

Grand Canyon National Park draws travelers from all over the United States and the world. Visitors always consider their means of transportation to and from the canyon. Historically, railroads have been developers in this country, and the Santa Fe developed and built most of the facilities for tourists. The U.S. government subsidized highway and airline travel in the form of federal highways and airports, but had nothing for the railroads. Their operations still had to come out of the corporate pocketbook. Instead, the government funded the railroad's competition.

In the mid-1920s, the roads to the park had not progressed beyond dirt and gravel. Two roads serviced the South Entrance. One originated in Flagstaff and the other in Maine (more commonly called Parks today). The National Park Service continually requested a paved road and a federal subsidy to do the work. As part of this process, they entreated Senator Carl Hayden to visit the park in order to determine the necessity for such a project.

The canny park service administrators invited him to visit during the monsoon season, knowing that if Hayden saw the roads in terrible shape the park would get the money. During this time of the year, heavy thunderstorms made the Maine road a quagmire. This is the route the senatorial party traveled with park service personnel as guides. It didn't take them long to get stuck axle deep in the mud. Several tows by handy teams of horses got them free and on their way, and the park got $100,000 the next year for a paved road from Williams to the Grand Canyon.

This highway subsidy was the beginning of the end for Santa Fe passenger service to the canyon. As automobile and airplane travel increased, the numbers of rail passengers decreased. As passenger revenues decreased, so did profits for Santa Fe stockholders. The Grand Canyon line had become a liability. Its days were numbered.

But it had not always been so. If any time can be called the golden days of the Grand Canyon Railway, the 1920s take the lead. Although no year ever saw 100,000 passengers cross the rails to the Grand Canyon, 1927 came the closest with 70,382. Even in 1953, when 20,000 Boy Scouts of America took the canyon by storm over an eight-day period, the total only reached 54,919.

||||||||||||||||||||||||

Class engine No. 1800, a 2-6-2 Prairie, waits at Grand Canyon station with the crew and station personnel for the last regularly scheduled Williams to Grand Canyon passenger run of World War II. Regular service was reinstated in 1946.

LAST GRAND CANYON R
Photo By Kolb Bro's

However, 1927 is also on record as the first year the number of automobile passengers entering the park exceeded the number of rail passengers. Autos brought in 7,048 more people than did the trains that year. To make matters worse, buses began regularly scheduled delivery of passengers to the gates of the park in 1928.

Automobiles gave people the freedom of choice. While traveling on federally built highways, people can stop whenever or wherever they please. Railroads run on a schedule. To ride a train, as pleasurable as it may be, one is required to travel at the convenience of the railroad and stop only when and where it stops. The combination of roads paid for by the government and the freedom of choice offered by the automobile proved to be more than railroad passenger service could withstand. Interestingly, today this circumstance is in the process of a reversal. Motor vehicles now choke the park's roads, and motorists are finding it more relaxing to ride the train. But the train will never exceed the numbers brought in by motor vehicles.

Buses were also more convenient to out-of-the-way towns and cities not serviced by railroads. As highways became more and more extensive, they enabled buses to skim away many previously loyal railroad customers. Small tour groups are more easily arranged for with buses. Special cars and trains are expensive and required larger numbers of people. Buses can pull up to any front door, load on forty people, and deliver them to the front door of their destination.

When airplanes first arrived at the Grand Canyon in 1933, another trend began that further eroded railroad passenger service on the Grand Canyon line. However, many years passed before air traffic to the canyon

Fred Harvey tour buses parked in front of the Desert View Watchtower, circa 1938.

resulted in a large number of visitors. Even by 1966, the total only reached 9,842 for the year.

But the precedent had been set. Federally funded projects for alternate means of transportation began the death knell for American railroad passenger travel. Federal subsidies for railroads did not come about until many had gone under or had drastically reduced both passenger and freight service. By then it was too late. Today's Amtrak, with its greatly reduced mileage and heavy subsidies, can barely compete. And now, due to proposed cutbacks in federal funding, it is in danger of extinction. The Grand Canyon branch of the Atchison, Topeka and Santa Fe Railway did not survive the corporate crunch.

Railway passenger service to the canyon drastically

declined in the two years preceding the beginning of the Great Depression. When the Depression hit late in 1929, revenue passenger totals dropped by more than 16,000 from the high in 1927. The skid continued until they hit rock bottom in 1933, with a total of 11,239 people transiting the line from Williams to the Grand Canyon.

Statistics for automobile passengers entering the park confirm the trouble yet to come. More people came in automobiles in 1933, the worst year for the railroad to date, than came by railroad in the best year of 1927. In 1933, 73,034 auto passengers checked in through the entrances to the park.

Buses didn't fare much better, but they did manage an increase in business. In this dismal year of 1933, 4,614 bus passengers came to see the wonders of the canyon. Remember too that this was the inaugural year of scheduled air service, with 107 first-of-a-kind passengers.

By 1932, Santa Fe management saw the writing on the wall. At the end of 1931, only 34,549 revenue passengers rode the train to the canyon. Up until that time, two scheduled trains made the daily trip in each direction, however the March 1932 schedule shows only one first-class passenger train for the daily round-trip. The cancelled train was the first casualty of the passenger crunch.

Up until then, there had been few changes in the train schedule except for arrival and departure times. In 1901, the schedule listed two trains: northbound number 10 and southbound number 11. An increase in traffic by 1905 dictated the addition of two trains, number 14 northbound and number 15 southbound. For some reason, in 1910 these numbers changed to 12 and 14 northbound and 11 and 15 southbound. And so it remained until the 1932 schedule change, with number 14 becoming the southbound and number 15 becoming the northbound. This last train numbering endured until July 30, 1968, with only the World War II hiatus causing a temporary change.

The lull from 1942 until May 30, 1946, had caused the printed schedules to show a blank space for the Grand Canyon District. The June 1946 schedule corrected this, and from that date until the September 1946 schedule appeared, the northbound train is listed as 124 and the southbound as 123. The September schedule returned to the numbers 14 and 15, headed in their original directions.

Over a period of years, several trains used numbers 123 and 124, but on the Grand Canyon line they became known as El Tovar. Originally they appeared on a summer supplementary train in 1940 that traveled from Kansas City to Los Angeles via the Grand Canyon. Round-trip service between Los Angeles and the Grand Canyon began in 1941 and continued through the war years until September 1946. Military personnel on recuperative leave made up a majority of the passengers during the war. El Tovar also picked up and dropped off cars at Williams for through service on other trains, usually trains 23 and 24. As published in the June 1946 schedule, consists included a sufficient number of the following cars: dormitory lounge, sleeping, tourist sleeper, dining, and chair. El Tovar disappeared from the schedules in 1946, and trains 123 and 124 disappeared with it until April 1950, when they appeared as the Grand Canyon Limited (the same name trains 23 and 24 ran under).

During the war years' break from scheduled passenger service, the weekly local made its regular Tuesday runs under the numbers 231 for the northbound and 232 for the southbound. Only one change is on the record: Tuesday operations switched to Wednesdays on June 1, 1959, for switching convenience in the yards.

All of these number changes had nothing to do with the operation of specials. Special trains, in as many sections as necessary, continued to visit the canyon over the years. Even after the discontinuation of scheduled passenger service in 1968, specials continued to make their way in and out of Grand Canyon Village along with the weekly local.

On September 17, 1951, the Grand Canyon line celebrated its golden anniversary. Fifty years prior, the first scheduled passenger train had made its way from Williams to the South Rim of the Grand Canyon. By 1951, problems with dwindling passenger revenues had become acute. Santa Fe records show only 34,377 paying passengers for the year. The previous year, 1950, had done considerably better, with 48,097. By 1954, revenues stabilized at about 35,000 per year. As most of these passengers traveled in the summer months of June through September, something had to give.

The first of November 1955 saw the first drastic change in the service offered by the railroad to the rim. On this day, Fred Harvey buses began the transfer of Santa Fe passengers from Williams to the canyon during the months of November through May. From 1956 until 1968, the scheduled buses ran from September 30 to May 25. This was instituted as a Santa Fe railroad service, with the passengers being ticketed from their point of origin through to the canyon. The buses merely operated under a lease agreement. The Fred Harvey Company had bought out the Santa Fe interests at the canyon

the previous year, except for the depot and yards. As this constituted railroad service, the Grand Canyon station remained the destination of the buses.

Curtailment of off-season train service helped the railroad's finances somewhat, but the losses continued to mount. By 1960, revenue passenger numbers dropped below the 10,000 mark, and by 1967 had gone off the charts to 4,658. Decision time for the board members of the Atchison, Topeka and Santa Fe Railway Company arrived in 1966. Even with the off-season reduction in service, passenger revenues at the 6,000 level could not justify the continuation of scheduled service to the canyon. When 1967 rolled around, they decided to shut down the railroad.

Considering some of the Santa Fe's cargo figures during this time, you get the idea rather quickly of the need for discontinuation. For this time period, 1961 was a typical year for service along the Grand Canyon branch. The following carloads were recorded to or from the indicated stations:

CARGO	RED LAKE	GRAND CANYON	WILLAHA	ANITA
Sheep and Goats	17	3	16	
Cattle			9	20
Feed			2	
Sand and Gravel		105		
Autos			2	
Oil and Gas			150	
Water		300	1	3
Petroleum Products	3			
Machinery	1			

Couple this meager traffic with 9,090 revenue passengers, and the picture is indeed bleak. Add figures in succeeding years of $6,730 in Pullman operation losses in 1965 and $7,622 in 1966, tack on figures for 1967 of a freight high of 22,444 tons in December and a low of 7,123 tons in August, then consider a passenger high of 2,200 in August and a low of 13 in March, and there is no other conclusion. The Grand Canyon branch barely made its diamond anniversary and would never see its seventy-fifth!

While the Santa Fe management considered these problems, a major east-west track realignment got under way. In 1960 and 1961, the company began and completed construction of a new double track north of the main line through Williams. Years of problems on the troublesome curves, grades, and tunnel of the existing main line through Johnson Canyon made this bypass a necessity. The new main line allows greater speed and safety. Along with the realignment came a new station.

When the new track went into service on December 19, 1961, station agent Glenn Irvin moved his office from the old Williams Depot and opened the new station shown on the timetable as Williams Junction. Now, the Grand Canyon trains bypassed Williams and added three miles each way to the run. The new station was east of Williams, and the canyon trains used the same north-south tracks plus part of the old main line on their new route. But this pleasant-looking station's days were numbered from the day it opened its doors.

When train 14 rolled into Williams Junction to end the tourist season on September 23, 1967, Santa Fe management planned to make it the last scheduled

passenger run of the Grand Canyon line. On April 25, 1968, the Atchison, Topeka and Santa Fe Railway Company notified the Arizona Corporation Commission by letter that they had no intention of continuing service from Williams Junction to the Grand Canyon in 1968, with lost revenues listed as their justification.

However, it did not end there. The commission held a hearing at the canyon in May and returned a finding that service was "reasonably necessary." A commission order on May 26 directed the railroad to resume service and continue through September 5, 1968. Santa Fe did in fact resume operations but tackled the problem in the Arizona Supreme Court. The court reversed the decision of the Arizona Corporation Commission and on July 24, 1968, ordered discontinuation of passenger service.

Without Emery Kolb to record the scene for posterity as he did the "Last Grand Canyon Run" in 1942, and without press coverage or even a fond farewell from a crowd of railroad personnel, train number 14 pulled out of the Grand Canyon for Williams Junction at 5:30 p.m. on July 30, 1968. A consist of diesel engine number 730 with one baggage car and one coach certainly did not make for a grand last train. Yet in its limited capacity, it represented almost sixty-seven years of passenger service history that has little parallel among this country's railroads.

Maybe engineer V. J. Conway thought of this as he gave the horn two short blasts and moved the throttle back to begin the last trip. Fireman J. E. Bland might have noticed the powerhouse and the laundry slide by with a bit of regret. It has gone unrecorded if any passengers rode on this last train, but one might assume at least a few did. As conductor J. D. Hart checked their tickets while the train gathered speed and moved out of the yards, he must have considered that this was the last time he'd take care of these duties on this run. Grand Canyon agent D. L. Burns thought about it, for he kept the original copy of the message terminating service and the clearance card. Conversation must have been at a minimum. What can one say when a way of life comes to an end?

The end came at Williams Junction with this notation on the dispatcher's train sheet: "No. 14 and 15 discontinued on arrival Williams Jct July 30, 1968." The time was probably about 7:15 p.m. No one came to say anything, for nothing more could be said. The statement on the train sheet laid Grand Canyon Railway passenger service to rest.

Specials, cattle extras, work extras, weekly freights, and ore shipments continued along the line for a few years on a helter-skelter as-needed basis. Ore shipments stopped in 1969, and cattle extras made their last appearance in 1973. Regular freights and all service to Grand Canyon stopped with the closure of the Grand Canyon station in 1969.

Early in 1969, when the Atchison, Topeka and Santa Fe applied again to the Arizona Corporation Commission to suspend all services to the canyon, no argument or court action ensued. Permission was granted. On May 13, a company message directed the closure of the Grand Canyon Depot at the end of shift on May 16, 1969. Agent Burns complied, but remained until May 20 to close out the business of the station. A subsequent message closed the station at Williams Junction on June 2, 1969. For agent Irvin, this routine brought no pleasure, as he had closed the Williams Depot and disposed

of its property eight years previously. These actions sealed both ends of a once vital railroad.

The roadmaster added a small footnote to train traffic on the line. In the summer of 1974, he decided to recover the usable track and materials along the right-of-way. The dispatcher sent two work extras in June for this purpose. On June 13, engines 3372 and 3441, with conductor P. D. Kirkland and engineer R. G. Long at the controls, took the section gang and a string of gondolas to the canyon in order to retire rail and fastenings. Then on June 20, conductor W. S. Peterson and engineer E. Sanchez made the trip north with engines 3402 and 3388 for the loaded material. As he notched the throttle back, engineer Sanchez had no idea he was operating what was to be the last Atchison, Topeka and Santa Fe Railway train out of the Grand Canyon. He did his job that sunny Thursday, and as far as he knew, there would probably be another train someday.

For many people, a way of life came to an end in 1974. No more passengers. No more ore trains. No more cattle extras. No more log trains. No more water trains. No more grand specials. People in Williams, along the line, and at the Grand Canyon became used to life without the railroad. Most believed the trains would never run again. In spite of these feelings, a revitalized Grand Canyon Railway returned. But it did not come quickly or easily.

If a railroad ever had a personality, it is the Grand Canyon line. Such a system should not be allowed to die. Several individuals tried to revive it as a tourist attraction in the late 1970s and early 1980s. All failed because they had no personal investment at stake in the project. These proposals of "I will run a railroad and make a fortune for myself if you will give me the money" just did not have a chance. Some people solicited funds from the federal government and sources other than their own. But with no personal investment, it was a no-go.

Then, in 1980, the Atchison, Topeka and Santa Fe filed with the Arizona Corporation Commission to abandon and salvage the Grand Canyon District. After all the legal dust settled, the commission granted the request and the Santa Fe contracted with a railroad salvage company to do the work.

Enter Railroad Resources, Inc., of Phoenix, Arizona. This company, which specialized in the leasing or sale of used rolling stock, salvage of railroad materials, dismantling of railroad properties, and railroad construction, took another look at the Grand Canyon line. President Charles Newman and Vice President Brian Alexander saw the potential for a revival of this line in the form of a vintage railroad tourist attraction.

When they contracted with the Santa Fe for the dismantling of the line in 1983, they had already looked at the road for one of the previous promoters. After completing several feasibility studies, checking their bank balance, and borrowing additional funds, on May 30, 1984, Railroad Resources purchased the right-of-way with options on the Fray Marcos Hotel, station in Williams, and other adjacent properties for the grand sum of $4,295,128. This purchase comprised 104 parcels of land for a total of 1,780.7 acres.

In March 1984, Railroad Resources ran a ballast regulator over the line from Williams to a point just outside of the park boundary. After clearing the weeds, brush, and small trees from the tracks, they assessed the cost to put the line back into operation. The rails remained in good shape, but many bolts needed to be replaced because the expansion and contraction from heat and cold had sheared them off. An estimated 20,000 ties needed to be replaced too before operations could commence, and a couple of small washouts and several bridge abutments had to be overhauled. Virtually all of the roadbed along the right-of-way and in the Grand Canyon yards needed reballasting. This work required several months.

The company stockpiled ties and spotted ballast cars in the yards at Williams. Brian Alexander identified for purchase fourteen clerestory roof eighty-six-seat coaches built by the Standard Steel Car Company from the New Jersey Transit Authority and ten Pullman-built Harriman-style ninety-six-seat coaches owned by the Southern Pacific. He conducted searches for motive power and considered several possibilities.

Vintage 1923 Pullman-built Harriman-style car being lifted onto a flatbed for transportation from Oakland to Richmond, California, for rebuilding of the trucks in January 1989.

The people of Williams began to gear up for a railroad. This looked like a serious venture, and after the false starts of previous promoters, people dared to hope again. Many doubters expressed their opinions but grudgingly started to come around. However, the president of Railroad Resources refused to relinquish controlling interest of the company in return for investment capital. Under these circumstances, potential investors wouldn't back the project. Under doubters' cries of "I told you so," Railroad Resources folded, and with it went the plans for the Grand Canyon line.

But the people of Williams were not ready to give up on the railroad yet. This project meant too much to the economy of the city. Ever since the Santa Fe stopped passenger service to the canyon and the railroad bypassed the city in the early sixties, the town's economy had entered a downward spiral. In 1984, the highway department completed the last link of Interstate 40, and it effectively killed Route 66 through the city. These two actions virtually sealed the town off from the traveling public. Several civic leaders worked hard to keep Williams from becoming a ghost town.

To them, the railroad was a vital part of the rehabilitation of the city's dying economy. They fought every attempt to scrap the line for steel and ties. Like a scene out of the Old West, when men and machinery arrived to salvage the tracks in town, the city marshal arrested the contractor for not having a permit and confiscated the equipment. This delayed them for a while, but they moved out of the town limits and ripped up one mile of ties from milepost 5 to 6.

Fortunately, in their search for funds a loan had been made to Railroad Resources by businessman Max Biegert. Foreclosure on the note gave him title to the upper twenty miles of track. After clearing the field of pretenders at a City Council–sponsored public meeting, Biegert determined the project to be feasible, purchased the remainder of the track and property, and began to run a railroad.

Max and his wife, Thelma, came up the hard way after his service in World War II. He scraped together all of the cash he could and began a crop-dusting business with a war-surplus Stearman and a lot of grit. They grew the business and did well in a worldwide aerial application business under the name Biegert Aviation International. Soon they added another family business, National Child Care. After finding themselves in the railroad business, they attempted to arrange additional financing for the project. But because of all the previous problems created by other promoters, the banks refused to consider their proposition. Max and Thelma then reached deep into their pockets, tapped other resources available to them, and came up with the $15 million necessary to get the first train to the canyon.

Assembly of a first-class team to make the project work was the next priority. Max took the reins as chairman and chief executive officer. Thelma, with experience earned from their business over the years, assumed the position of secretary-treasurer. Robert Roth came on board as president and chief operating officer with many years of recreational business acumen gained in the trenches at Holiday Inn and Del Webb. Brian Alexander's extensive civil engineering and railroad experience made his selection as vice president of railroad operations and construction a natural choice. These four principals formed the nucleus of the team.

Original Grand Canyon Railway staff in front of the Grand Canyon Depot at the January 10, 1989, announcement for the rebuilding of the line. **LEFT TO RIGHT:** Lois Klein, public relations; Bob Roth, president; Thelma Biegert, secretary-treasurer; Max Biegert, chairman; Brian Alexander, vice president; Al Richmond, historian-museum curator.

All through 1988, the officers and consultants conducted feasibility studies, planned, located and purchased equipment, hired key personnel, and formulated a plan of action. On January 10, 1989, at the historic Grand Canyon Depot, the company principals announced the plan with a major press conference. "The Grand Canyon Railway is for real. Operations will begin with a steam train from Williams to the Grand Canyon on September 17, 1989, the eighty-eighth anniversary of the first passenger train in 1901," they said. The media gave the project good coverage across the country. Skeptics abounded, but in short order their tune changed as they watched the company progress and build.

Work began concurrently on the tracks, engines, cars, and the renovation of the Fray Marcos Hotel and depot in Williams. The company's goal was to launch the reinaugural train and open the facilities to the public on September 17. Scheduled as the southern terminus of the line, the Fray Marcos would be revived from its status as a derelict building to one of prominence within the city of Williams. Already on the National Register of Historic Places as the largest and oldest poured concrete building in Arizona, the Fray Marcos is the southern anchor of this historic railroad.

The principals outlined plans that called for a spur line to the Grand Canyon airport at Tusayan, two hotels, an Old West theme park, and maintenance facilities. It was estimated the project would cost $80 million and take up to eight years to complete. Management agreed early on to make this a truly first-class historical project. To that end, they included in the plans a museum that would be open to the public free of charge, displaying vintage equipment and artifacts.

It's difficult to imagine a more hectic period than January to September 1989. The company literally began with nothing more than a derelict building, sixty-four miles of weather-beaten track, and a nucleus of people. Within nine short months, everything had to come together. To accomplish these seemingly impossible tasks, Biegert and his team built an even larger team of experts.

Roadmaster John James hired on and assumed responsibility for rebuilding the right-of-way. To do so required locating and purchasing 30,000 ties, finding track equipment, and hiring the best available men to do the work. James used his years of railroad construction experience and contacts to locate people of

the highest qualifications. Retired Santa Fe division engineer "Tex" Garland reported in as the maintenance-of-way consultant. He had been responsible for the Grand Canyon line during his employment with the Santa Fe. Retired Santa Fe bridge and building foreman Cliff Gipson (with fifty-four years of railroad experience) served the Grand Canyon Railway as railroad bridges and structures consultant. Sam Imbleau and John Morris headed up the track gangs. These men and their gangs worked long, hard days through the spring and summer in order to make the deadline.

Work began at milepost 5 on March 29 with the replacement of one mile of ties stolen from the roadbed.

||||||||||||||||||||||||||

ABOVE LEFT: The Fray Marcos Hotel on March 29, 1989, the day restoration began. Note the advanced state of deterioration.

LEFT: A surfacing machine works on the depot track one week before opening. Note the new windows of the same design as when they were first installed on the refinished exterior of the Fray Marcos and the original 1908 brick platform.

BELOW: Williams Depot and Fray Marcos Hotel in 1984. The ballast regulator to the right had been run over the line in the preliminary survey done by Railroad Resources.

Track gangs and bridge and building crews coordinated their schedules and began the sixty-four mile march to the South Rim. In a little over five months, the track gangs walked this distance several times in the course of their work, and the bridge and building crew visited every bridge and culvert. They pulled and replaced ties, rails, beams, and spikes by the thousands. As they completed the basic work, ballast trains followed behind the crews, replacing the volcanic cinders that had been depleted by years of erosion. Ballast regulators and surfacing machines then made the final adjustments by tamping ballast, leveling, straightening the tracks, and finishing the surface. On August 1, the crews reached the yards at the Grand Canyon, and September 14, they presented Max Biegert with a twenty-four-carat gold spike maul to celebrate a first-class right-of-way for the Grand Canyon Railway.

Grand Canyon Railway GP-7s on company tracks under their own power for the first time, on April 26, 1989. **LEFT TO RIGHT:** Bob Roth, president; Max Biegert, chairman; John James, roadmaster; Al Richmond, historian; Gary Bensman, chief mechanical officer; Brian Alexander, vice president; Will Ambrose, engineering consultant.

Chief mechanical officer Gary Bensman faced a task that on the surface defied common sense. Where, in 1989, would they find the vintage locomotives and qualified steam personnel needed to run this line? The enginemen (and -woman) turned out to be the least difficult. Bensman, with his extensive back-

Newly resurfaced tangent track south of Red Lake station just a few days before the running of the reinaugural train on September 17.

ground in the twilight world of American scenic steam railroads, knew most of these people, at least by reputation. They came from as far as Georgia (in the person of master mechanic Robert Franzen). Enginemen came from all over: Phil Eskew from Arizona, Ervin White from Connecticut, Mike Ramsey from Colorado, Kent McClure from Illinois, Russ and Marty Fischer from New Mexico, and Robert Crossman and Charles Harris from Texas. Retired Santa Fe engineer Will Ambrose, with over thirty years of experience with steam and diesel, served as the Grand Canyon Railway locomotive consultant. His experience included design engineering with the Baldwin Locomotive Works and service as a locomotive engineer on the Grand Canyon line. Three

Ambrose generations were destined to serve on this railroad. Will grew up in Williams while his father worked for the Santa Fe as a conductor, and his son Roy became a brakeman with the company.

Alexander had already done considerable scouting of motive power and rolling stock, but Bensman and Biegert had to travel and inspect them for purchase. This travel literally took them halfway around the world, for China seemed to be the best bet for vintage locomotives in good running condition. Negotiations for the purchase of several American Baldwin locomotives had progressed reasonably well when student unrest and the massacre in Tiananmen Square caused a government upheaval that made further dealings impossible.

Other purchase or lease arrangements then became necessary, and finally the company purchased four vintage 1906-10 Alco 2-8-0 consolidation-type locomotives in July. Numbers 18, 19, and 20 came from John Slack's Lake States Steam Transportation Company at Laona, Wisconsin. Steve Mattox of Council Bluffs, Iowa, who owned number 29, also agreed to sell. Originally built for the Lake Superior and Ishpeming Railroad, numbers 18, 19, 20, and 29 hauled iron ore from their date of delivery until 1960. Then sold to the Marquette and Huron Mountain Railroad, 19 worked the scenic line and the others remained in storage until 1985, when they were sold to Slack and Mattox. Company crews prepared all four for the move to Arizona and did some additional work on number 18 in Laona. Owing to some delays caused by the Chicago and North Western, the engines did not arrive in Williams until late in August.

It seemed an impossible task to have number 18 ready for service on September 17. But with a thorough

No. 19 from the livery of the Lake Superior and Ishpeming Railroad. Built in 1910 for the LS&I by Alco, she served on that line until 1960. The Grand Canyon Railway later declared the locomotive to be surplus and sold her to the MGM theme park in 1993.

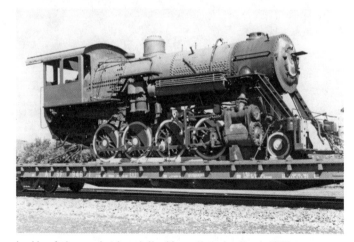

Looking forlorn and stripped, No. 18 awaits unloading in Williams on August 20, 1989.

Two Grand Canyon Railway tenders and No. 20 pass by Flagstaff's station on August 27, 1989, en route to Williams. The loads required 100-ton flatcars.

knowledge of their craft and a willingness to work twenty-hour days, the enginemen had her rolling at 1:23 a.m. that day. Testing had to be completed in the early morning hours in time to couple her to the passenger cars waiting in the station at 11:30 a.m. for a noon departure. Volunteer assistance also played a part in getting 18 ready for the big day. Staff, family, and friends helped with the detail painting of the wheels, running boards, and windows, and with polishing the brass bell and whistle. This relieved the enginemen for the more skilled mechanical work. For everyone involved, it was an incredible feat of stamina and workmanship.

Passenger cars had been selected by Alexander during his time with Railroad Resources. The seventeen 1923 vintage Pullman-built Harriman-style cars came from the Southern Pacific yards in Oakland. They needed a complete overhaul and refit due to their advanced state of disrepair and decay. Car superintendent Bryan Reese selected seven in the best condition and arranged for their transport to the Tucson car shops of Pacific Fruit Express. The remainder went to Richmond, California, for overhaul and eventual shipment to Williams.

After the cars arrived in Tucson on April 15, Reese hired foreman Greg Griffin and work crews to complete the necessary stripping and rebuilding of the rolling stock. As with the locomotive, the cars had to be ready by September 17. The crew removed all furnishings, windows, fixtures, and electrical systems and then sandblasted years of paint and rust from the exteriors. Metal repair and preparation for painting followed. After exterior painting in the Pacific Fruit Express shops, the cars needed a new electrical system and windows, wood refinished, interior painted, and seats reupholstered

Thelma and Max Biegert on the pilot of No. 29 the day it arrived in Williams. No. 29 entered into revenue service during the 1990 season.

and reinstalled. The hard work paid off when the cars, complete with "Grand Canyon" painted in gold letters, arrived in Williams on September 10.

From the beginning, bricks and mortar were an integral part of the overall plan. Building construction and rehabilitation moved forward concurrently with work on the locomotive and cars. The Fray Marcos Hotel and depot had been allowed to deteriorate into derelict status. Considerable work needed to be done. A new engine and car repair facility also began to take shape, along with fuel and water storage tanks.

The Fray Marcos and depot presented a challenge. Tim Rogers, director of construction, established his crews, hiring carpenters, concrete workers, electricians, equipment operators, masons, plumbers, and welders. Because the building is on the National Register of

Historic Places, salvage and preservation of the remaining artifacts and significant building components were vital. Almost all of the furnishings and fixtures had been sold off by the Santa Fe when the buildings were retired, but several documents guided restoration. Exterior and interior walls required sandblasting to remove years of grime and paint. In this process, the original layers of 1908 paint resurfaced, allowing restoration crews to replicate the building's color scheme. The wooden windows had deteriorated too much to salvage them. Modern metal sashes were constructed to look exactly like their wooden forebears. Tons of cinders were removed from the flat concrete roof so a peaked roof could be constructed to handle the winter snows and monsoon storms. Rehabilitation began on March 29 and continued right up to the time of opening.

New construction of the engine and car facility began at the same time along the main line on the north side of town. Many tons of concrete had to be poured for the floors and drop pits used to service the power and rolling stock of the line. As the building took shape, rails were laid into and through it from the main line. Welders using cranes and a spider web of scaffolds put together the steel 760,000-gallon water storage tank just to the north of the engine and car facility. After installation of a water-softening unit, the tank was filled with effluent water piped from the Williams water treatment plant to the west of the main line. For conservation of the area's most precious resource, the company's steam locomotives would use reclaimed water from Williams and the Grand Canyon. The facility became operational in December, but the water tank lasted only until early in 1992, when it collapsed because of faulty

Newsboys pass out copies of the *Territorial Times* on the day of the reinaugural run. The headline tells the story.

welding. Water is now treated and pumped directly into water cars and tenders.

Because of health problems, Rogers had to step down from the position of director of construction in July. Paul Vorachek succeeded him and brought this phase of construction to completion.

Beyond reconstruction of the railroad and equipment, a major facet of the overall operation was the marketing and sales of the railroad's services. Concurrent with the rebuilding, others developed the sales program, reservations center, special promotions, and the media campaign. Regularly generated news releases to newspapers, TV, and radio allowed the public to follow the progress of the railroad. On the opening day of the reservations center, staff received over 200 calls. By the

The Grand Canyon Railway logo welcomes passengers and visitors to the depot in Williams.

Under a lowering sky and a cloud of red, white, and blue balloons, No. 18 pulls out of the Williams station at noon on September 17 for the reinaugural run to the Grand Canyon with honorary engineer Will Ambrose at the controls.

middle of September, the fall inaugural season, lasting from September 18 to January 1, was nearly sold out. Additionally, group bookings of 7,000 passengers had been made for the 1990 season. The sales and special programs required logos, brochures, tickets, flyers, and signs. Gini Alexander focused on this work and produced all of these items, usually with little notice and impossible deadlines.

Media interest increased daily as the locomotives and coach cars arrived. Coverage of the revived line appeared in nearly every major daily newspaper and on most television and radio networks. International magazines and newspapers from Switzerland to Japan also carried news of the grand reopening.

It all came down to the wire in the last few hours of September 17. Ten thousand people and dignitaries,

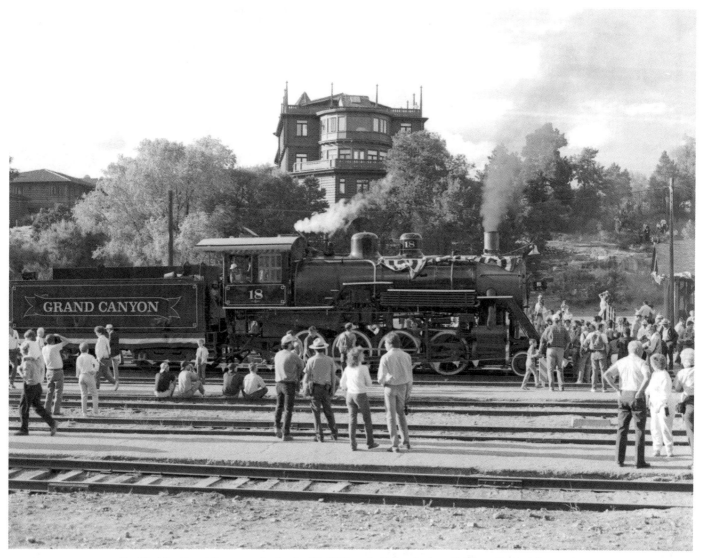

No. 18 at the Grand Canyon on September 17, 1989, rests in the shadow of El Tovar Hotel while crowds gather around for a look at the first steam locomotive to enter the yards since 1953.

including Arizona governor Rose Mofford, arrived in Williams to cheer on the "Little Train That Could" and celebrate Arizona's newest railroad. All morning long, under a lowering sky, bands played and dignitaries made their congratulatory speeches. But everyone kept looking to the east. Down the track, number 18 sat with wisps of smoke curling up from the stack and mechanics continuing to work feverishly on her. Somehow, the mechanical force managed to create the miracle. At 11:30 a.m., 18 backed into the station and coupled onto the newly refurbished coaches. In the age-old tradition, Thelma Biegert christened the engine with champagne and the riders scrambled through the crowds to get on board. At 12:01, engineer Will Ambrose notched the throttle back and the train inched forward. In this moment, the Grand Canyon Railway began its second life.

Today's passengers ride comfortably in 1923 Harriman-style chair cars and 1950s vintage dome, parlor, and chair cars. They listen attentively to steam engines barkin' or the growling of the diesels as they work up a grade. Many take pleasure in the mournful echoes of the steam whistle or the raucous diesel air horns at a grade crossing. Those echoes take them back to the past.

During the 1950s, a mountain lion waited for the train every morning around milepost 35 and sat patiently beside the tracks, hoping the crew would throw it scraps of food. She has long since disappeared. That whistle is a reminder of the cries of the big cat who waited so many years for these trains to return.

It is also a reminder of the railway's visionary.

Because of his date with destiny in the Spanish-American War, Buckey O'Neill could not ride the first train to the canyon in 1901. I like to think his spirit rides in the cab of every train headed to the canyon today, walking the cars to greet the passengers. Even from the afterlife, O'Neill would want to be a part of the new Grand Canyon Railway, to share his dream with the newer generation of visitors.

Hang on, Buckey! Here we go again!

The former Santa Fe overpass near Prescott tells another story. Although abandoned, the Grand Canyon line never completely went away.

Grand Canyon Railway No. 18 makes its way into Grand Canyon during a snowstorm in 1989. The first winter of operation produced some of the heaviest snowfalls and lowest temperatures recorded in many years. In spite of these difficulties, the railroad managed to keep an on-time schedule.

THE SECOND 100 YEARS

HEN THE FIRST GRAND CANYON Railway train left the Williams Depot, it began a twelve-year odyssey that in 2001 brought this pivotal railroad to its centennial celebration of passenger service to the Grand Canyon. Even today, the railway can only be considered a work in progress. Its perpetual constant is change.

For the remainder of 1989, work continued on facilities, equipment, and the right-of-way. Operations maintained a daily train schedule through January 1, 1990, and then shut down for two months to catch up on needed work. Mechanical crews worked feverishly in the new locomotive and car shop during those two winter months to bring number 18 completely up to standards and finish the major overhaul on number 29 begun in September. Built in 1906 and larger than 18, she had been selected to become the second steam locomotive on the fledgling Grand Canyon Railway.

Although number 18 was considered operational, many corners had been cut in the short time allowed to make her serviceable for the reinaugural run. During the remainder of the 1989 season, she experienced many mechanical problems with consequent downtime. This necessitated frequent use of Grand Canyon Railway's two GP-7 diesels to head up the daily trains in her place. In fact, her problem began with the reinaugural run. Due to overheated bearings, the train arrived late at Grand Canyon and number 18 spent the night in the yards with mechanics working feverishly all night to get her under way. The diesels made the return run with the celebrants and brought the next day's train to the canyon. Number 18 then reoccupied her rightful place at the head of the train for the return trip to Williams.

Motive power problems, both steam and diesel, plagued the railroad for the remainder of the first year. In order to give mechanics an opportunity to complete scheduled inspections and spend sufficient time correcting defects, the company occasionally leased diesel locomotives from the Santa Fe. For the first time since

1974, Santa Fe Geeps in blue and yellow livery made their appearance on the line. And for something different, GP-20 number 2736 from the aborted Southern Pacific Kodachrome livery, in red and yellow, made several runs at the head of Grand Canyon Railway trains.

While the motive power struggles continued, seven additional coaches with overhauled trucks arrived from Richmond, California. Some entered the shops for rehabilitation and others became a source of spare parts. In order to provide upgraded service, one coach underwent extensive modification. After the removal of several rows of seats in the center section, company carpenters built a first-class mahogany bar complete with a mirror; this became the Grand Canyon Railway club car. Throughout the following twelve years, all of the cars underwent several modifications to include public address systems, metal entry Dutch doors, and roller bearings, which replaced the original, less-efficient friction bearings. These improvements made the cars more serviceable, safer, and more comfortable for the passengers.

Infrastructure improvements also remained a priority. Throughout the remainder of 1989, work on rolling stock continued without protection from the elements. As winter set in, this created additional hardships for the mechanical staff. Completion of the shop became an immediate objective. Begun in March, the work required considerable time, expense, and effort. Although the exterior is basically a simple structure, the shop it encloses includes an overhead crane, drop table for removing drivers and trucks, and an extensive array of machine tools. Many of these tools came from railroad machine shops around the country as some of the major lines downsized. All of them required proper installation and setup.

The Grand Canyon Railway club car was the company's first upgraded piece of rolling stock. The mahogany bar was handcrafted by company carpenters.

On January 15, 1990, the crews moved out of the wintry northern Arizona weather into a modern, well-heated shop. When they rolled numbers 18 and 29 inside, the mechanics not only had a relatively comfortable place to work, they also had arguably the best steam locomotive shop in the country. Here, they could work with proper tools in a far safer environment and manufacture the parts needed to make their ancient charges fit for service again. In later years, these walls witnessed the most extensive rebuilding of a steam locomotive in the latter half of the twentieth century. Without a proper and well-equipped shop, it could not have been accomplished.

At the same time, work continued on the depot and historic Fray Marcos Hotel. Original plans called for the company offices to be located on the second floor in what had been the guest rooms. However, this was not to be.

Built in 1907–08 of poured concrete reinforced with rails, all of the plumbing and utilities had been buried in the walls and were not accessible. Modern building codes made rehabilitation of the structure uneconomic. Restrooms, for instance, would require a completely separate addition to the building. When all was said and done, after extensive modification, the first floor became the trainmaster and dispatcher offices, the museum, and a waiting room. To date, a considerable part of the second floor is only usable for storage. Company offices continued to operate out of rented quarters in downtown Williams into the middle of 1994.

Throughout the first winter, the track gang continued their efforts to provide the railroad with a first-class right-of-way. They only slowed down when weather made work impossible. In five and a half months, they had achieved a major accomplishment. These hardworking men had reclaimed a sixty-four-mile derelict roadbed and turned it into a smooth class-one right-of-way.

But much remained to be done. After they changed out 30,000 ties, the crews needed to replace another 10,000 each year. Their work is a never-ending process that requires replacement or realignment of rails and fittings; improvements on drainages, bridges, and culverts; and the addition of sidings and other tracks. Routine maintenance includes daily track inspections prior to train departures. During the dry season, they become firefighters, following the trains to prevent wildfires caused by occasional sparks from the locomotives.

After the initial rebuilding, their first major project began on April 30. The Grand Canyon Railway needed

The Grand Canyon Railway track gang has kept the railroad running in all kinds of weather and has also managed to upgrade the right-of-way. Here, they remove a turnout from the main line at Willaha to extend the siding another 400 feet.

a passing track and a place to load ballast. Willaha, at milepost 37.8, is approximately the halfway point between Williams and the Grand Canyon. In 1905, the Santa Fe established a 1,900-foot siding there as a cattle- and ore-loading station (it was retired in 1974). This proved to be the best location for the new siding.

The track gang began construction as soon as the southbound evening train passed that day. They had positioned pre-built turnouts at the south and north ends of the siding, and when the train cleared the south end, the men went to work ripping out the main line rails and ties. As soon as they leveled the roadbed, front-end loaders hooked onto the south turnout and dragged it into place. Next, they bolted the turnout into the main line, then ballasted and leveled it to first-class standards. The very next evening, this skillful crew repeated the scenario for the north end, and over the next two months they completed the job between all of their other scheduled projects.

By the spring season of 1990, number 18 had been outshopped after completion of a major overhaul, and she opened the daily schedule on March 1. With number 29's rebuilding nearing completion, steam motive power prospects began to look up.

Once a major part of the railroad's history, specials had ceased to run to the canyon in 1969. A wonderful return to this tradition came in the form of a Santa Fe special on April 4. The company presidential special sported five Budd stainless steel cars headed up by FP-45 numbers 100 and 101 in the reborn Santa Fe Warbonnet red, yellow, and silver livery. Santa Fe president Michael Haverty ran this reinaugural train from Los Angeles to Chicago with a stopover at the Grand Canyon. Grand Canyon Railway engineers and a conductor had the pleasure of piloting this first foreign train.

Three days later, two Grand Canyon Railway trains

Dignitaries have always been a part of the Grand Canyon Railway. Today's line is no exception. Arizona Governor Rose Mofford dedicated the railway and museum, and here takes part in the "hanging" of a train robber from a handy telegraph pole.

Senator Barry Goldwater became a regular visitor to the railroad. During a 1990 visit, he exchanged books and autographs with Al Richmond at the Williams Depot.

began daily service. Known as the Buckey O'Neill Special and the Williams Flyer, trains 1, 2, 5, and 6 departed at 8:00 and 10:00 a.m. and returned at 5:00 and 7:00 p.m. daily, except for Christmas Eve and Christmas Day. Number 18 ran at the head of the first train, and Santa Fe GP-30 number 2769 headed up the second train until number 29 was outshopped. On April 26, number 29 entered revenue service, and the Grand Canyon Railway ran two steam trains that day for the first time.

This season became a time of celebration. On April 28, railfans ran up Kodak's stock when numbers 18 and 29 became the first Grand Canyon Railway steam doubleheader to run the line. To make it even more special, the railroad's first distaff engineer, Marty Fischer, ran number 18 with her husband Russ as fireman. Further

cause for celebration came when former senator Barry Goldwater christened number 29 on Cinco de Mayo. A man of style, he disdained champagne on this anniversary of the Mexican Army's unlikely victory over French forces at the Battle of Puebla on May 5, 1862. He chose tequila as a more appropriate medium of baptism. He rode the Grand Canyon Railway several times before his death in 1998.

Innovation also became a part of this season. Earlier in the year, Arizona governor Rose Mofford again rode the train with her staff. To welcome Arizona's chief executive, Williams marshal John Moore rounded up a bunch of local cowboys and staged a holdup of the train

Marshal Goodmore stands with desperados of the Cataract Creek Gang in the daily Wild West show at the Williams Depot. He has triumphed over the villains in more than 10,000 of these gunfights.

at milepost 3. Riding up to the train, the "robbers" brought it to a halt, boarded, and proceeded to rob the passengers. As part of their ill-gotten gains, they collected a souvenir watch from the governor complete with her likeness on the face. After a fierce shoot-out, the marshal captured the robbers. With ropes looped over a telephone pole and around their necks, the hapless robbers pleaded with the governor for their lives. Her response? "Hang 'em!" Governor Mofford's watch

But the Cataract Creek Gang is a tough bunch. Later in the day, they have revived and are seen holding up the train.

continues to grace the Arizona State Railroad Museum, which she supported as a board member until she passed away in 2016.

That day also marked the birth of the Grand Canyon Railway's world-famous Marshal John B. (be good or be gone) Goodmore and the notorious Cataract Creek Gang. Since June 30, 1990, they have performed daily Wild West shows and train holdups to the delight of travelers from around the world. Originally the shootouts took place on the brick platform, but that became more and more painful to those unfortunate owlhoots who "lost" the gunfight with the always-faster marshal. Over the years, their lot slowly improved with different prepared sets, first on the east end of the depot and now on the west end, where they have a first-class set complete with bleachers for the spectators. One year they shared the set with a buffalo calf that eventually became

too difficult and dangerous to handle.

Train holdups are the stuff of legends, and the Cataract Creek Gang is establishing its own with daily robberies at several locations along the line. They stop the train, ride alongside shooting it up, board, and rob everyone on board. Of course, the marshal arrives in the nick of time and to the delight of the passengers, captures the gang, and hauls them off to the hoosegow. "They went that way" is the frequent helpful cry of youngsters who are more than willing to be one of the marshal's deputies. Kids, adults, and especially foreign riders all have marvelous stories to tell when they get home about the "Great Train Robbery" in the Wild West.

Entertainment on the train also settled into a regular pattern. Originally, entertainers varied on a day-to-day basis, rotating among cowboy musicians, Indian dancers, Mariachi bands, and singers. By popular acclaim, the cowboy musicians eventually surfaced as the most appreciated. Two, Paul Karlsberger and Kevin Johns, are the most enduring. Both sing popular Western and railroad ballads to self-accompaniment on either banjo or guitar. They stroll the entire train going to and from the canyon, serenading the passengers, who frequently sing along. This allows them to claim that they have "walked" to and from the canyon more than anyone else.

The museum also came of age during this first year. The curator and four staff members from the Sharlot Hall Museum in Prescott, Arizona, loaned many of the artifacts and installed them just prior to the reinaugural. For the remainder of 1989 and into 1990, the Grand Canyon Railway curator collected and organized artifacts relative to the Grand Canyon Railway, mining, ranching, logging, and the Fred Harvey Company into interpretive displays. The curator returned the loaned Sharlot Hall displays on August 6, 1990, and installed exhibits that eventually became the Arizona State Railroad Museum. During the first anniversary celebration on September 15, Governor Mofford formally dedicated the museum with a ribbon-cutting ceremony.

Throughout these years, many people who visited the museum have donated artifacts, photographs, and memorabilia. Often, contributors want to remember family members' contribution to America's railroads. This theme continues to be the focus of the Arizona State Railroad Museum.

Grand Canyon Railway's gift shop is one of the more successful aspects of the company. It became so successful that the company doubled its size by 1995. Later, in 1999, they added an equally successful annex in the Grand Canyon Railway restaurant. Travelers are delighted by the wide assortment of clothing, books, model trains, railroad memorabilia, art, jewelry, and other quality merchandise.

On September 29, the celebration continued with the longest Grand Canyon Railway train of the year. Eleven cars left the station behind doubleheaded numbers 18 and 29. A railfan special left earlier behind GP-7 number 2072 in her new "stealth" livery in all black. It made several stops for photo run-bys en route and then waited at Willaha for the regular train to catch up. Engines then switched trains, and 18 continued with the railfan special for run-bys in Coconino Canyon. This gave railfan and regular passengers the thrill of seeing both steam and diesel trains and a doubleheaded steam train all in one day.

Then, just prior to Christmas, on December 17,

Grand Canyon Railway No. 18 southbound out of Grand Canyon passes Bright Angel overlook.

after thirteen months of operations, the Grand Canyon Railway hosted its 100,000th passenger. In its first year, it had already exceeded the Santa Fe's best year by more than 20,000 riders. It was a fine Christmas present and a harbinger of things to come. The railroad ran its last train of the season on January 1, 1991, and welcomed a new year.

During the first year of operations, several changes of key personnel occurred. Most notably, President Bob Roth and Vice President Brian Alexander both tendered their resignations and moved on to other opportunities. During this time, chief mechanical officer Gary Bensman also departed the company. These and other changes all came about during a general reorganization and assessment of priorities. In the years to come, the company found it very difficult to attract and retain quality people for a wide variety of reasons. They included the rural location, poor working conditions, and mismanagement at supervisory levels. The poor working conditions became better with improved facilities, but it took several years for the management problems to be resolved.

During these trying times, Chairman Max Biegert assumed the duties of president until May 1991, when Marshal Bryant became the company's new executive. Formerly the Grand Canyon Railway's chief financial officer, he brought a different style of leadership and helped the company begin its long struggle to profitability. In 1995, roadmaster Bob LaCivita was promoted to director of operations, and that branch of the company began to take a turn for the better. But other changes in the company's hierarchy loomed on the horizon. When 1997 rolled around, Bryant moved on to other pursuits and David Chambers stepped in as president. With a long and strong business background, he reorganized much of the company's business practices and objectives and shepherded the Grand Canyon Railway into the twenty-first century. Although administrative and personnel changes continued, railroad operations improved and the mechanical department continued to add rolling stock to the roster.

The most notable event of the third operating year came on the heels of the season opening date, February 1, 1991. Scarcely three weeks later, the railway began its most ambitious undertaking since the reinaugural. On February 21, locomotive 18, with a consist of one tank car for water and three Harriman coaches, entered the

The Hassayampa Special at Phoenix Union Station. Brand-new Santa Fe GP-60-M No. 144 in Warbonnet livery faces off with its eighty-year-old predecessor.

Santa Fe main line at 7:31 a.m. to join up with Santa Fe GE Dash 8-40B number 7445. So began the odyssey of the Hassayampa Special from Williams to Phoenix and the return of the Santa Fe's Peavine. Virtually all of the Grand Canyon Railway's trainmen would participate in this historic trip by making the run in relays.

The first passenger train on the Peavine since the Santa Fe discontinued service in 1968, the Hassayampa Special evolved as a means to gather additional publicity for the Grand Canyon Railway. Its destination was Phoenix, to help celebrate Phoenix Union Station Days, sponsored by the National Association of Railroad Passengers. In this mission, it more than succeeded. Newspapers around the country reported on the trip, and Arizona television crews followed the train in motor vehicles and helicopters. Cameramen also rode the train and filmed inside the coaches and cab of the steam locomotive. Their video and interviews made the national news.

After leaving Williams, the train began the steep descent down the grades to Ash Fork with SF 7445 providing dynamic braking. At Ash Fork, the Dash 8 disconnected, and the train continued south across the high bridge of Hell Canyon to Skull Valley, where the local fire department helped pump water into the tender and tank car. A pre-positioned fuel truck replenished the oil supply, and after servicing the engine, the crew completed the last leg of the day to Wickenburg. Here the crew repeated the drill of watering, fueling, and servicing with the help of Wickenburg's fire department and tied up the train for the night.

Bright and early the next morning, the special moved out of Wickenburg's station in a circus atmosphere en route to Phoenix. Railfans followed the train all along the highway, and television station helicopters flew in formation or circled. Crowds of onlookers and dignitaries who wanted to catch a glimpse of the first steam train to arrive at Union Station in almost forty years attended the arrival in Phoenix at 3:07 p.m.

For the next two days, number 18 sat nose-to-nose with Santa Fe's new GP60B number 144, in Warbonnet livery. Crowds thronged the station and admired the displays of past and present locomotives along with Amtrak and private passenger equipment.

With slightly less media coverage, the Hassayampa Special began the return trip up the Peavine to Williams at 9:32 a.m. on February 25. Crews again serviced and

Diesel and steam side by side in the Grand Canyon Railway shop. The newly acquired FPA-4 went through several months of work in a complete rebuild from traction motors to exhaust stacks.

tied up the train at Wickenburg for the night. As number 18 had to work harder up the grades of the Peavine, servicing again took place at Skull Valley and also Ash Fork. When she rolled into Williams at 3:57 p.m. on February 26, number 18 and the Hassayampa Special had scored an impressive public relations victory by letting the whole nation know the Grand Canyon Railway had made a successful return with steam passenger service to the Grand Canyon.

Later that year, the railway reached another motive power milestone. Former Canadian National Railway (VIA) Alco FPA-4 number 6773 arrived at Williams on October 20 in a snowstorm. Deadlined since 1989, 6773 became the first of what would be Grand Canyon Railway's impressive fleet of Alcos. She required extensive mechanical, electrical, and exterior work that kept her from revenue service until the following year.

After a month off in January for mechanical work, the railway began the 1992 season on February 1. Seven days later, the railroad's first upgrade, the club car, entered revenue service. Four days later, Grand Canyon Railway added its first passenger car since the original purchase of seventeen coach cars in 1989. The Chief Keokuck entered revenue service as the railway's parlor car. Complete with a rear platform, this car provided luxury service for riders who wanted to relive the best years of railroad passenger service. This car differed from its company-owned companions in that it had been leased from the Keokuck Junction Railway.

The remainder of 1992 and 1993 proved to be very active years for all departments of the railway. The track gang built a new 910-foot spur at Quivero, but during the winter several wet storms kept them busy repairing washouts. January and February turned out to be the wettest on record. The worst storm took out seventy feet of track at milepost 21.5. This necessitated returning the southbound train to Grand Canyon, where more than 200 passengers were loaded onto buses for the return trip to Williams. Many hours of hard work throughout the night by the track gang allowed the train to return in time for the morning run to the canyon.

Later in the year, one of the original four steam locomotives found a new home. Once it had been declared surplus to the needs of the railroad, shop personnel

||||||||||||||||||||||||||||

The last and only time that all four of Grand Canyon Railway's original steam locomotives were brought together for a group photograph. They stand at the north end of the railroad's shop with Bill Williams Mountain in the background.

cosmetically restored number 19 and loaded it onto 100-ton flatcars for the journey to Las Vegas. Sold to the MGM theme park, it became a static exhibit that also served to advertise the Grand Canyon Railway. The company also declared GP-7 number 2072 to be surplus and thus ended its short-lived career as one of the railway's first locomotives on property.

During these years, train schedules changed and special trains began to appear on the line more frequently. The primary change in scheduling caused the removal of the Buckey O'Neill Special as a daily train. From this point on, only the Williams Flyer remained on the schedule, but second sections were added when passenger counts required another train. One such instance occurred when the pope visited Denver. To accommodate several Vatican and Arizona church dignitaries and their staff who wished to visit the Grand Canyon en route to Denver, on August 19, 1993, the Vatican Special, with Alco number 6773 in the lead, headed north as the second section of the Williams Flyer.

In the coming years, other specials made regular appearances, but with a new wrinkle. Motive power for these trains usually came from the Amtrak roster. The first of these, the National Park and Conservation Association special, entered the Grand Canyon Railway main on May 12, 1994, with a brand-new Genesis number 812 in the lead, trailing private cars Monterey, Bela Vista, and Montecito. This was quite a colorful train, but nothing compared to the first American Orient Express to run the line on July 20, 1995. Headed up by Amtrak F40PHs 406 and 334, twelve beautifully appointed cars carried their passengers to the South Rim in luxury never before witnessed on the line. The

American Orient Express made several regular appearances on the Grand Canyon Railway every year until its demise in 2008.

By this time, the railway outgrew its office space in Williams and had great difficulty keeping reservations agents and quality accounting staff. Most agents attended Northern Arizona University, and a majority of the accounting staff lived in Flagstaff. This necessitated a daily sixty-mile drive that could be quite hazardous in the winter. The company packed up its administrative, operations, marketing, accounting, and reservation staff and moved them to new quarters in Flagstaff. Mechanical, train, and track personnel continued to operate out of Williams. In Flagstaff, the railway occupied offices on the first and second floors of the Aspey, Watkins and Diesel Building and the second floor of the historic Federal Building on San Francisco Street.

These offices eventually became too costly, and the company again moved everyone, on January 30, 1998, to a one-floor suite of offices on West Route 66 in Flagstaff. This location also improved staff access to Williams via I-40 and provided sufficient parking.

The next major phase of the Grand Canyon Railway finally came to pass on January 19, 1995. After a year of planning, construction began in Williams on the new Fray Marcos Hotel. Located just to the north of its historic counterpart, this eighty-nine-room first-class hotel became the centerpiece of the Grand Canyon Railway campus. Construction moved right along, and on July 28, Max and Thelma Biegert welcomed their first guests.

In addition to first-quality rooms, the hotel lobby features fine wood and stonework, original Western art, bronze statuary, and comfortable seating around a roaring fireplace. Just off the lobby is Spenser's Lounge, which features an imported century-old English bar and clock along with additional regional artwork.

George Spenser handcrafted the oak bar in 1887 for the Lion's Den pub in the small village of Shepherd's Bush, England. For 200 pounds and the promise that he would never have to buy another drink in the Lion's Den, Spenser worked day and night for four months to create his masterpiece. He apparently made a good bargain, as he lived to see his eighty-fourth year and visited the pub daily. The Biegerts found the bar in New Orleans and had it shipped to Williams in time for the grand opening of the new Fray Marcos.

The hotel proved quite successful, and in 1999 the company began construction of a 107-room addition, complete with a swimming pool. This second phase of hotel expansion opened its rooms to occupancy on Feb-

The finished product, Grand Canyon Railway No. 4960 gleams in the setting Arizona sun the evening before entering revenue service.

ruary 12, 2000. A third phase addition of 102 rooms opened to the public in March 2004.

An integral part of the company's plans for a full-service facility, the restaurant began construction in 1998 and opened its doors on March 4, 1999. Complete with a 300-seat dining room, banquet room, and gift shop, Max and Thelma's Restaurant serves breakfast, lunch, and dinner to railroad guests, travelers, and local folks.

Several significant additions to motive power and rolling stock occurred in the second half of the 1990s. Former Chicago, Burlington and Quincy Mikado number 4960 entered into revenue service on July 27, 1996, after a dedication ceremony marking the most extensive rebuilding of a steam locomotive in the second half of the twentieth century. The railway also added several

Derelict and forlorn, former Chicago, Burlington and Quincy No. 4960 rests in the weeds at the Grand Canyon Railway shop after her trip from Michigan.

new diesel units to the company roster. All ex-VIA, A units 6762, 6768, 6788, 6793 and B units 6860 and 6871 joined 6773 to bring the motive power roster total to four steam and eight diesel locomotives.

After complete overhauls of the three units, the Grand Canyon Railway ran its first A-B-A set in revenue service on October 16, 1998. This initial run included units 6793, 6871, and 6773. In their distinctive livery of railroad green, gold, and red, they were the only operational A-B-A sets in the country at that time.

Also, to assist in providing electrical power and steam heat to the train, the Grand Canyon Railway has acquired two ex-VIA power cars. Equipped with electric and steam generators, these cars are capable of supplying all power needs to the train irrespective of head end power.

New cars began to make regular additions to the roster during these years. The Grand Canyon Railway's first dome car, Coconino, arrived after years of service with the Northern Pacific and Amtrak. Hot on its heels came the former CN business car Bonaventure, which, after a complete interior renovation, became the line's parlor car, the Chief. When the Chief entered revenue service, the Chief Keokuck was returned to its owners at Keokuck Junction.

Other first-class cars also made their appearance. After refurbishing, the former Southern Pacific chair car number 2377 became the Anasazi. Former Pennsylvania Railroad parlor/drawing room number 7132 became the café car, which in addition to the café features a gift shop. The first dome car proved so successful that the railway acquired a companion dome car, the Kokopelli. Actually, there have been two cars by this name. The

Grand Canyon Railway dome car Coconino and parlor car Chief en route to the Grand Canyon.

first, a leased former Chicago, Burlington and Quincy and Amtrak dome car, ran in revenue service in 1999 and 2000. When the owner cancelled the lease, another leased Kokopelli entered revenue service in 2000 after extensive interior renovation. Its origins are with the Great Northern, Burlington, Spokane, Portland and Seattle, and Amtrak. First-class chair car Colorado River is the latest addition. Formerly a Denver Rio Grande Western sleeper, it later became a coach for the Chicago and North Western. Not only did it change in configuration, it began service as the Silver Aspen and then became the Iowa River. After a complete mechanical and interior renovation, it again changed names and entered revenue service on April 20, 2000.

One particularly unusual piece of rolling stock ran the line in 1997. In an effort to convince park service planners of the feasibility that light-rail could alleviate traffic problems within Grand Canyon National Park, the Grand Canyon Railway hosted a Siemens Regio Sprinter for a conference scheduled at the South Rim.

One of the more unusual pieces of rolling stock to be seen on the Grand Canyon Railway, the Siemens Regio Sprinter crosses a bridge northbound for the Grand Canyon.

On January 30, an Amtrak special train brought the two-unit Sprinter on 100-ton flatcars into the Grand Canyon Railway yards, where crews unloaded it. It then made its way to the canyon under its own power.

The next day, attendees of the Grand Canyon forum on transportation in the park made several trips around the yards. Two hundred riders, including Secretary of the Interior Bruce Babbitt and Grand Canyon National Park Superintendent Rob Arnberger, took advantage of the opportunity. Also available were two buses that National Park Service bureaucrats believed would be the transportation of the future for the park. Some rode the electric bus, but it promptly broke down. After Babbitt and Arnberger rode the train, they immediately recognized the advantages of light-rail over buses, and it became the primary consideration for transportation of visitors into and within the park.

Four years later, as costs escalated and visitation to the South Rim flattened out, politicians became involved in the process and light-rail disappeared from consideration. Visitors to Grand Canyon continue to battle traffic congestion, parking problems, and hordes of buses creeping around the South Rim. Now buses at the park are electric or propane powered. Most people with knowledge of light-rail know its benefits as more environmentally sensitive, economical, comfortable, and convenient. Light-rail has the added incentive of being aesthetically pleasing to the general public in comparison to buses. However, the politicians and bureaucrats have prevailed, and it appears that buses at Grand Canyon are here to stay.

Specials, celebrities, and dignitaries continue to ride the Grand Canyon line. In addition to Burlington Northern Santa Fe business trains and the American Orient Express, the Great American Station Foundation Whistlestop Tour train, two American Association of Private Railroad Car Owner specials, regular National

Grand Canyon Railway motive power lineup in the Grand Canyon yards, LEFT TO RIGHT: 1910 No. 18, 1959 No. 6773, and 1923 No. 4960.

Railway Historical Society railfan specials, and the Bill Gates special are among the wide variety that have visited the park via the Grand Canyon Railway.

Bill Gates's train caused a stir in Williams and at the canyon. The beautiful vintage Wisconsin and Southern Railroad train set with E-9As in the lead was enough to turn anyone's head. But when people learned that Bill Gates and Warren Buffett, two of the world's wealthiest men, were on board, that really got their attention. Taking advantage of the opportunity, the Cataract Creek Gang held up the train but had to go from car to car before they found their victims engaged in a card game. Marshal Goodmore saved them in the nick of time but "arrested" Bill Gates for gambling and hauled him off to the pokey by the ear.

The private car owners bring in the most unusual and colorful specials. They consist of cars from virtually every railroad across the continent. These specials quite commonly include restored passenger service cars from the Santa Fe, Chesapeake and Ohio, Seaboard, Great Northern, Union Pacific, Canadian National, Southern Pacific, Canadian Pacific, Rock Island, Wabash, Frisco, and Wyoming and Pacific, to name a few. In addition to their railroad of origin, they carry names that evoke memories of places such as Glacier Park and Cimarron River. Others have wistful names like Scottish Thistle and Silver Lariat. No matter the name or railroad of origin, they're all beautiful.

Celebrities and dignitaries no longer ride the Grand Canyon Railway in the numbers of days gone by, when the railroad served as the primary means of access to the national park. However, Grand Canyon Railway continues to host those who have found the train a

⁗⁗⁗⁗⁗⁗⁗⁗⁗⁗⁗⁗⁗⁗⁗⁗⁗⁗⁗
One of the first American Orient Express specials backs into the Grand Canyon Depot with Amtrak "Pepsi can" No. 503 in the lead.

The court of flags at the entry to the Grand Canyon Railway Williams Depot and the new Fray Marcos Hotel. The American flag is flying at half-staff in honor of those killed in the attack of September 11, 2001.

better way to visit. Senator Barry Goldwater, Arizona governor Rose Mofford, entertainers Kenny Rogers, Glen Campbell, and Ernest Borgnine have all made more than one trip. Even in today's high-speed world of politics and entertainment, there are those who still enjoy the more leisurely means of travel as offered by today's railroads.

Without the rights-of-way and the track workers who build and maintain them, no scenic railroad can operate. The Grand Canyon Railway is no exception. Since the line reopened, it has continually improved its condition and responded to emergencies. To date, these men have literally rebuilt the right-of-way and added considerable lengths of track.

With more than 7,000 feet of additional track, they created new sidings at Apex, Willaha, and Quivero,

lengthened shop and yard tracks, and built a new yard tracks. These major construction projects came about while workers were also keeping up with routine maintenance and nature's rampages. In an effort to outdo the 1993 storm, on August 19, 2001, a super cell thunderstorm settled in over milepost 16 and washed out forty feet of track. This caused the southbound train to stop at Quivero and the railway to launch a massive response to the emergency.

Track crews immediately began work on the damaged section. By working through the night, they managed to get the train into Williams in time for the morning run to the canyon. In the meantime, employees were marshaled to ferry the passengers to Williams in a variety of buses and vans while others prepared and delivered food to those still on board. Hostlers and carmen went to Quivero to prepare the train for the next day's service. When the passengers boarded the train on the August 20, they had no idea what had transpired the previous night.

Shopmen and carmen are also the unsung heroes of the railroad. Working long hours, they constantly struggle to keep the railroad's rolling stock in operating condition, rebuild and upgrade equipment, and meet inspection deadlines. The age and variety of equipment boggles the mind, and yet somehow they manage to keep it all in good order.

Due to the high cost of steam operation and maintenance, the company found itself having to cut back on the number of steam trains. In a cost-cutting measure, management decided to run steam from Memorial Day to the first weekend of October. Diesels head up the trains for the remainder of the year. Both are historic and accurate for the Grand Canyon line. The steam locomotives date from 1906 to 1923, and the diesels date to the 1950s. Over the years, the Santa Fe ran steam, diesel, and steam-diesel consists in regular service. Today's Grand Canyon Railway continues that tradition.

The operations department hires on or trains its crew members. They usually begin as brakemen, work their way up to fireman and/or conductor, and some eventually become engineers. Firemen and engineers learn the rules of operation and the road on the diesels and then progress to the more complicated steam locomotives. There have been two women who qualified as diesel and steam engineers, and others may follow.

Sadly, after a difficult battle, roadmaster Sam Imbleau succumbed to cancer in 2001. In recognition of his dedication to excellence in everything he did for the Grand Canyon Railway, the company changed the station name at milepost 52 from Apex to Imbleau. Nothing could be more fitting, since Apex is a high point on the line and a reporting point. Henceforth, Sam's name will be called out with every train that passes. The new name was first reflected in timetable 10.

Change on the Grand Canyon Railway has been constant. It continued when Max and Thelma decided to retire and sold the railroad lock, stock, and railroad spike to the Xanterra Corporation in 2007.

Today, more than 100 years after Buckey O'Neill began his efforts to bring a railroad to the South Rim,

Six days after the terrorist attack on the United States, Grand Canyon Railway owners and personnel observe the 100th anniversary of the railroad. A far cry from the planned festivities, this demonstrated that the American spirit was alive and well.

the Grand Canyon Railway endures. But it has not been without cost and difficulty. Fortunately for the traveling public, the environment, and history, today's Grand Canyon Railway continues to serve the grandest of canyons. In greater numbers than ever before, travelers arrive at the South Rim refreshed, entertained, and eager to witness nature at its best. Their decision to leave their vehicles in Williams and ride the train bodes well for the environment. And maybe best of all, their very presence ensures that Buckey's efforts were not in vain and history continues to be made on the Grand Canyon Railway.

GLOSSARY

This partial list of railroad terms and slang covers only those used in this text. Several good, complete glossaries are available for readers interested in learning the language of the railroader.

AIR BRAKE: Brakes operated by air pressure

AIR MAN: A hoghead with better than average feel for the use of air brakes and the control of the train

BLOCK: Designated length of track between signals

BOILER: Metal tank in which water is converted to steam by heat from the firebox

BOOK OF RULES: Handbook of company rules and regulations

BRAKEMAN: The person who operates manual brakes on individual cars and throws switches

CAB: Control compartment of a locomotive, with the engineer on the right and the fireman on the left

CLEARANCE: Authorization for train movement

CONDUCTOR: Person in charge of a train

COUPLER: Heavy steel mechanism at both ends of cars and locomotives for connecting them together

DINKEY SKINNER: Engineer for a logging railroad

DIRT TRACK: Roadbed without ballast

DIVISION: Part of a railroad under the control of a superintendent and the location of a crew change stop

DYNAMIC BRAKE: Locomotive brake system using a conversion of momentum into heat by electrical means, which in turn retards the speed of the locomotive

ENGINE: Another word used for locomotive; actually the power component of a steam locomotive

EXTRA: Train not listed on the printed schedule

GANDY DANCER: Track worker; this name came from the use of Gandy Company track tools

GRAB IRONS: Hand railings on rolling stock used as a handhold during mounting or riding on the side

HIGHBALL: Hand or oral signal to move a train and also used to indicate "moving fast"

HOG: A locomotive

HOGHEAD: Locomotive engineer; the person trained to run a locomotive

HOSTLER: Person who services locomotives and moves them about the yard

IN THE DITCH: Train that has been wrecked

JOIN THE BIRDS: To jump from a moving engine or car, usually just prior to a wreck

LOCAL: Freight train that sets out, picks up, and switches cars in a given area or district

LOCOMOTIVE: Power unit of a train; for steam, it consists of an engine and a tender

ON THE GROUND: Off the tracks; derailed power or rolling stock

PASSING TRACK: Siding to allow passing of trains on a single-track main line

PILOT: Wedge-shaped metal barrier at the front of a steam locomotive and at both ends of a diesel to push aside obstacles on the track, also called a cowcatcher

POWER: General term for locomotives

RAIL: One of a pair of steel bars that make up a railroad track for the purpose of providing a running surface for the wheels of locomotives and cars

RELAY RAIL: Rail removed from one location and relaid at another location; salvaged rail

ROAD: Main line track

ROADBED: Bed upon which the ties, rails, and ballast of the railroad track lies

ROADMASTER: Division officer responsible for keeping the track in his division in good repair

ROLLING STOCK: All wheeled equipment used on a railroad track

SCHEDULE: Printed timetable that gives number, class, direction, and route for a train

SECTION: One of two or more regular trains running on the same schedule; it can also mean the length of track to be maintained by a section gang

SECTION GANG: Crew of track workers used to maintain a specific length or section of track

SHOOFLY: Temporary bypass track around damaged or obstructed track

SIDING: Track adjacent to the main line, usually with a switch at both ends, for the purpose of passing trains (passing track) or setting out rolling stock

SINGLE TRACK: Main track on which trains are operated in both directions

SPOT: Position a piece of rolling stock for work, loading, or unloading

SPUR: Track with only one switch from the main line

STATION: Place designated by name in the schedule

SWITCH: Rail device with movable rails used to turn rolling stock from one track to another

TENDER: Storage component of a locomotive that carries fuel and water

TORPEDO: Explosive device placed upon the rail to warn an approaching train of danger ahead

TRACTIVE FORCE: Energy transferred from the locomotive's drivers to the rails

TRAIN: Coupled rolling stock operating under orders

TRUCK: Wheel-axle assemblies upon which power and rolling stock rests and which causes it to be guided along the rails

TURNOUT: Switch

UNIT: Complete diesel-electric locomotive or support section to a lead unit

VARNISH: Passenger train, from the days of varnished wooden cars

WORK EXTRA: Train with materials and equipment for maintenance or construction

BIBLIOGRAPHY

PERSONAL INTERVIEWS

Acosta, Jose A., Atchison, Topeka and Santa Fe Railway Section Foreman, Flagstaff, Arizona

Alexander, Brian K., Former Vice President, Grand Canyon Railway, Flagstaff, Arizona

Ambrose, Wilfred G., Baldwin Locomotive Works Design Engineer, Atchison, Topeka and Santa Fe Railway Locomotive Engineer, Phoenix, Arizona

Babbitt, John G., President, CO Bar Livestock Company, Flagstaff, Arizona

Baker, Bob, General Manager, Train Operations, Grand Canyon Railway, Williams, Arizona

Biegert, Max L., Chairman and CEO, Grand Canyon Railway, Williams, Arizona

Biegert, Thelma, Secretary-Treasurer, Grand Canyon Railway, Williams, Arizona

Black, John L., Coconino County Deputy Sheriff, Longtime Resident of Williams and Flagstaff, Arizona

Black, Vera Goss, Teacher, Longtime Resident of Grand Canyon, Tusayan, and Williams, Arizona

Blair, Cherrie L., Rancher, Lifelong Resident of Williams and Valle, Arizona

Blair, David F., Rancher, Lifelong Resident of Williams and Valle, Arizona

Bradley, John D., Head of Grand Canyon Mule College, Longtime Resident of Grand Canyon, Arizona

Cartledge, Thomas R., U.S. Forest Service Archaeologist, Kaibab National Forest, Arizona

Chacon, Thomas R., U.S. Forest Service District Ranger, Kaibab National Forest, Arizona

Chambers, W. David, President, Grand Canyon Railway, Flagstaff, Arizona

Chappell, Gordon S., National Park Service Western Regional Historian, San Francisco, California

Christman, Warren C., Atchison, Topeka and Santa Fe Railway Communications Technician, Williams, Arizona

Cook, Martha K., Grand Canyon Railway Passenger, Flagstaff, Arizona

Corona, Gil, Atchison, Topeka and Santa Fe Railway
Section Hand, Williams, Arizona

Cravey, Mary Lockridge, Lifelong Resident of Grand
Canyon, Anita, and Williams, Arizona

Curry, George G., Atchison, Topeka and Santa Fe
Railway Field Engineer, Williams, Arizona

Davis, John H., Superintendent, Grand Canyon
National Park, Arizona

Duffield, George A., Atchison, Topeka and Santa Fe
Railway Maintenance, Escondido, California

Flohrschutz, Gene, Atchison, Topeka and Santa Fe
Railway Regional Manager, Public Relations, Los
Angeles, California

Fuller, Lester H., Cattleman, Sheepman, Lifelong
Resident of Northern Arizona

Garland, Robert G., Atchison, Topeka and Santa Fe
Railway Division Engineer, Phoenix, Arizona

Gipson, Clifford G., Atchison, Topeka and Santa Fe
Railway Bridge and Building Foreman, Phoenix,
Arizona

Gipson, Marie Burbank, Atchison, Topeka and Santa Fe
Railway Telegrapher, Phoenix, Arizona

Hadder, Eric M., Chief Mechanical Officer, Grand
Canyon Railway, Williams, Arizona

Irvin, Glenn W., Atchison, Topeka and Santa Fe
Railway Stationmaster, Williams, Arizona

Kuhn, Millard E., Secretary-Treasurer, Arizona Lumber
and Timber Company, Flagstaff, Arizona

LaCivita, Robert, Vice President, Operations, Grand
Canyon Railway, Flagstaff, Arizona

Lanter, Samuel L., Chief Mechanical Officer, Grand
Canyon Railway, Williams, Arizona

Lauger, William, U.S. Forest Service Landscape

Architect, Kaibab National Forest, Arizona

Macauley, Michael P., Northern Arizona Rancher,
Coconino County Deputy Sheriff, Longtime Resident
of Williams and Flagstaff, Arizona

Mann, Walter G., U.S. Forest Service Supervisor, Kaibab
National Forest, Arizona

Matson, Harry E., Lifelong Resident of Apex and
Williams, Arizona

McCallister, Michael, Santa Fe Field Engineer, Williams
and Flagstaff, Arizona

Melick, Dermont W., Santa Fe Doctor, Longtime
Resident of Williams, Arizona

Moore, Grace Lockridge, Resident of Grand Canyon,
Anita, and Williams, Arizona

Newman, Charles R., President, Railroad Resources,
Inc., Phoenix, Arizona

Nicholas, Daniel A., Fred Harvey Company Fire and
Safety Supervisor, Grand Canyon, Arizona

Oswald, William E., Educator, Longtime Resident of
Williams, Arizona

Pearson, Helen, Author, Lifelong Resident of Williams,
Arizona

Perrin, Lilo M., Northern Arizona Rancher, Lifelong
Resident of Williams, Arizona

Plese, Sonny J., Atchison, Topeka and Santa Fe Railway
Engineering Technician, Winslow, Arizona

Polson, Kenneth M., Fred Harvey Company Bus Driver,
Lifelong Resident of Williams, Arizona

Pouquette, Marjorie H., Teacher, Lifelong Resident of
Williams, Arizona

Riker, David F., Burlington Northern Santa Fe Railway,
Director of Administration, Arizona Division,
Winslow, Arizona

Roth, Robert I., Former President, Grand Canyon Railway, Williams, Arizona

Samson, Pauline J., Teacher, Lifelong Resident of Williams, Arizona

Sandoval, Juan, Atchison, Topeka and Santa Fe Railway Section Foreman, Williams, Arizona

Schmitz, Eugene L., Atchison, Topeka and Santa Fe Railway Locomotive Engineer, Winslow, Arizona

Setterland, John, Saginaw and Manistee Lumber Company Locomotive Engineer, Williams, Arizona

Smith, Robert W., Atchison, Topeka and Santa Fe Railway Hostler, Cowboy, Lifelong Resident of Williams, Arizona

Spivey, Mahlon E., Atchison, Topeka and Santa Fe Railway Roadmaster, Phoenix, Arizona

Stephenson, Ken, Trainmaster, Grand Canyon Railway, Williams, Arizona

Sullivant, R. Howard, Businessman, Lifelong Resident of Williams, Arizona

Sutton, William B., Atchison, Topeka and Santa Fe Railway Locomotive Engineer, Justice of the Peace, Williams, Arizona

Thurston, Leland E. ("Bill"), Cattleman, Miner, Businessman, Longtime Resident of Tusayan, Arizona

Turner, Eloise Fain, Teacher, Author, Longtime Resident of Grand Canyon and Clarkdale, Arizona

Verkamp, John ("Jack") G. Jr., Businessman, Lifelong Resident of Northern Arizona, Grand Canyon, Arizona

Wadsworth, Manley, Atchison, Topeka and Santa Fe Railway Section Hand, New Oraibi, Arizona

Wamble, John T., Atchison, Topeka and Santa Fe Railway Station Agent, Williams, Arizona

Way, Thomas E. ("Spike"), Author, Justice of the Peace, Longtime Resident of Williams, Arizona

White, Ervin H., Trainmaster, Grand Canyon Railway, Williams, Arizona

Wilson, Woodrow E., Saginaw and Manistee Lumber Company Commissary Supervisor, Flagstaff, Arizona

CORRESPONDENCE

Arizona Bureau of Geology and Mineral Technology, Geological Survey Branch, Tucson, Arizona

Arizona Heritage Center, Historical Repository, Arizona Historical Society, Tucson, Arizona

Chamberlin, Edward M., National Park Service Museum Technician, Grand Canyon, Arizona

Gehrt, Robert E., Atchison, Topeka and Santa Fe Railway Assistant Vice President, Public Relations, Chicago, Illinois

Glover, Vernon J., Southwestern Historian, Albuquerque, New Mexico

Mallin Brothers Iron and Metal Company, Scrap Dealers, Phoenix, Arizona

Martin, Michael A., Atchison, Topeka and Santa Fe Railway Manager of Public Affairs, Los Angeles, California

Menninger, Constance L., Santa Fe Archivist, Kansas State Historical Society, Topeka, Kansas

Moore, John B. Jr., Railroad Historian, Albuquerque, New Mexico.

Myrick, David F., Author, Railroad Historian, Santa Barbara, California

Rees, David I., Railroad Historian, Ajo, Arizona

Shine, Joseph W., Author, Railroad Historian, La Mirada, California

Torpin, Q. W., Atchison, Topeka and Santa Fe Railway General Manager, Los Angeles, California

Wahmann, Russell, Author, Railroad Historian, Cottonwood, Arizona

PUBLICATIONS AND ARCHIVES

Arizona Department of Mineral Resources, Phoenix, Arizona.

Arizona State Archives, Phoenix, Arizona.

Atchison, Topeka and Santa Fe Railway, 1897–1921. Contracts, correspondence, and documents. Topeka: Office of the Secretary-Treasurer.

———, 1902. *Titan of Chasms: The Grand Canyon of Arizona*. Chicago: Passenger Department.

———, 1908–1985. *Santa Fe Employees Magazine*. Los Angeles: Public Relations Department.

Baldwin Locomotive Works, 1906. *The Atchison, Topeka and Santa Fe Railway System: Record of Recent Construction #56*. Philadelphia.

Bradley, Glenn D., 1920. *The Story of the Santa Fe to 1920s*. Boston: The Gorham Press.

Burpee, C. Miles, 1945. *Railway Engineering & Maintenance Cyclopedia*. Chicago: Simmons-Boardman Publishing Corp.

California State Railroad Museum Library, Sacramento, California.

Chappell, Gordon S., 1976. "Railroad at the Rim: The Origin and Growth of the Grand Canyon Village." *Journal of Arizona History* 17: 89–107.

Cline, Platt, 1976. *They Came to the Mountain*.

Flagstaff: Northern Arizona University.

Coconino County Assessor, Flagstaff, Arizona.

Coconino County Recorder, Flagstaff, Arizona.

Coconino Sun (Flagstaff, Arizona), 1891–1978.

Darton, N. H. et al., 1916. *Guidebook of the Western United States, Part C, The Santa Fe Route*. Department of the Interior and the U.S. Geological Survey Bulletin 613.

Fuchs, James R., 1953. *A History of Williams, Arizona 1876–1951*. Tucson: University of Arizona Bulletin 23.

Gamst, Frederick C., 1980. *The Hoghead*. Boston: Holt, Rinehart and Winston.

General Soil Map, Coconino County, Arizona, 1972. U.S. Department of Agriculture, Soil Conservation Service.

Gornitz, V., and P. F. Kerr, 1970. "Uranium Mineralization and Alteration." *Economic Geology* 65: 751–68.

Grattan, Virginia L., 1980. *Mary Colter; Builder upon the Red Earth*. Flagstaff: Northland Press.

Hay, Oliver P., 1922. "Descriptions of Species of Pleistocene Vertebrata 5: Collection of Fossil Mammals Made at Anita, Coconino County, Arizona." *Proceedings of the U. S. National Museum* 59: 617–38.

Higgins, G. A., 1901. *Grand Canyon*. Chicago: Atchison, Topeka and Santa Fe Railway Company.

Hughes, J. Donald, 1967. *The Story of Man at the Grand Canyon*. Grand Canyon Natural History Association.

———, 1978. *In the House of Stone and Light*. Grand Canyon Natural History Association.

James, George Wharton, 1900. *In and Around the Grand Canyon*. Boston: Little, Brown and Company.

Kansas State Historical Society, Topeka, Kansas.

Koch, Michael, 1971. *The Shay Locomotive: Titan of the Timber*. Denver: World Press, Inc.

Lindsay, E. H., and N. R. Tessman, 1974. "Cenozoic Vertebrate Localities and Faunas in Arizona." *Journal of the Arizona Academy of Science* 9: 3–24.

Muir, John, 1902. "The Grand Canyon of the Colorado." *Century Illustrated Monthly Magazine*, November: 107–16.

Museum of Northern Arizona, Flagstaff, Arizona.

Nations, J. D., and Edmund Stump, 1981. *Geology of Arizona*. Dubuque: Kendall/Hunt.

Nations, J. D., J. J. Landye, and R. H. Hevly, 1982. "Location and Chronology of Tertiary Sedimentary Deposits in Arizona: A Review." In *Cenozoic Nonmarine Deposits of California and Arizona*: Pacific Section, edited by R. V. Ingersoll and M. O. Woodburn, 107–22.

Northern Arizona University, Cline Library Special Collections and Archives, Flagstaff, Arizona.

Richmond, Albert J. Jr., 1987. *Historic Precipitation Sequences on the Colorado Plateau, 1859–1983*. Master's thesis, Northern Arizona University.

Scarborough, Robert B., 1980. "Breccia Pipe Sources." *Fieldnotes* 10, no. 4: 3–4.

———, 1981. *Radioactive Occurances and Uranium Production in Arizona*. Report prepared for USDE by the Arizona Bureau of Geology, 43–50.

Sharlot Hall Museum, Prescott, Arizona

Smith, Jack, 1984. *Tales of the Beale Road*. Flagstaff: Tales of the Beale Road Publishing Company.

Suran, Charles W., 1989. *With the Wings of an Angel*. Unpublished manuscript.

U.S. Department of the Interior, Bureau of Land Management. Phoenix: Government Land Office Maps and Surveyors Field Notes.

U.S. Geological Survey. Maps and surveys. Flagstaff, Arizona.

Waesche, Hugh, 1933. "The Anita Copper Mine." *Grand Canyon Nature Notes* 7: 108–12.

Way, Thomas E., 1980. *Summary of Travel to the Grand Canyon*. Prescott: Prescott Graphics.

Williams News, 1886–1901. William Sullivant private collection.

Williams News, 1886–2006.

Wisbey, Herbert A., 1946. *The History of the Santa Fe Railroad in Arizona to 1917*. Master's thesis, University of Arizona.

Worley, E. Dale, 1965. *Iron Horses of the Santa Fe Trail*. Dallas: Southwest Railroad Historical Society.

PHOTO CREDITS

AL RICHMOND retired from Air Force Pararescue
as a chief master sergeant in 1981 after twenty-
seven years of service. Al then served as Colorado
Plateau projects liaison to the national parks and
monuments in his twenty-year second career with
Northern Arizona University. He is the founder
and currently chairman and CEO of the Arizona
State Railroad Museum Foundation in Williams,
Arizona. A nationally recognized historian and
author with an emphasis on railroads and the
Colorado Plateau, he has served as historian for
the Grand Canyon Railway since its rebirth. Al
lectures on the Colorado Plateau, climate history,
transportation history, and the American Civil War.
Published in history journals and periodicals, he is
also the author of *Rails to the Rim: Milepost Guide
to the Grand Canyon Railway* (eight editions) and
co-author with Marc Pearsall of *The Grand Canyon
Railway: Sixty Years in Color* (two editions).